MW01624750

Praise for Stand Out!

"The heroes we want to model are more than high performers at work. They understand themselves, exhibit leadership with integrity and compassion and have meaningful relationships. And typically they've been around a while. But here's a clear guide for attaining that notable success in your 30s or even 20s. Nathan's concise principles create a clear plan to authentically be the 'Young Professional Employee Every Organization Wants.' This is the book I wish I had coming off the farm many years ago."

– DAN MILLER
New York Times Bestselling Author of *48 Days to the Work You Love* and host of the *48 Days* Podcast

"Nathan Magnuson is a leader compelled by the unshakeable desire to serve others… he was born to help people grow! In his most recent book, *Stand Out!*, Nathan brings his trademark candor and freshness to the day-to-day realities faced by young professionals around the world. His advice is born of experience and his wisdom forged in the trenches of the modern workplace. This book should be required reading for new employees, and probably all the others, at every organization."

– MARK MILLER
VP, High Performance Leadership, Chick-fil-A, Inc. & International Bestselling Author of *Chess Not Checkers*

"There are leadership books with great sounding theories and then there are ones with practical advice designed to propel action. *Stand Out!* is the latter. Not only does Nathan share lessons learned from his own leadership experiences, he coaxes readers to look both inward in reflection and outward toward creating a richer, more meaningful tomorrow, for themselves and others. This book is an excellent field manual for young professionals who wish to accelerate their personal and professional growth."

– JANET KAMERMAN
Executive Assistant Director (retired),
Federal Bureau of Investigation

"*Stand Out!* provides many significant insights for young professionals looking to gain a leg up in their early careers – lessons I learned through trial and error on my own career journey. The need to expedite the development of young professionals to take on significant leadership roles has never been greater, and Nathan continues to be a trusted thought leader in making this a reality."

– ERIC EVANS
CEO, Surgery Partners, Inc

"This is a message every young professional needs. In a culture characterized by blame, entitlement, and indecision, *Stand Out!* stands out! Success begins with personal accountability and as Nathan writes, you're never too young to set a good example. Thank you for encouraging our young professionals, Nathan!"

– JOHN G. MILLER
Author of *QBQ! The Question Behind the Question*

"In a world where job possibilities are endless, Nathan helps equip young professionals with tools necessary to get them into their zones of excellence. Life should be a ruthless pursuit of purpose and Nathan helps young people fulfill both passions and professions!"

– CHRIS TUFF
Bestselling Author of *The Millennial Whisperer*

"Nathan's message for young professionals *stands out!* As CEO of a company that supports thousands of emerging professionals every year, I believe there is no more important endeavor today than to equip young professionals to be more self-aware, purpose-driven leaders. Nathan's simple, clear lessons on self-awareness, commitment to purpose and leadership do exactly that!"

– DANIEL JACOBS
CEO, Avanoo

"*Stand Out!* is both timeless and timely. Nathan Magnuson harvests powerful insights from the literature on leadership development and crafts them into a very accessible guide to growing as a young professional. The book's timeliness comes from his experience as a Millennial professional and his keen observation of peers and bosses. His conclusions and recommendations ring true for the 2020s!"

– ROBERT J. THOMAS
Author of *Crucibles of Leadership* and Executive Director (retired), Accenture Institute of High Performance

"Some of the most important questions are the ones we ask ourselves. When you have supported emerging leaders for several decades, as I have, you learn that none of us has all the answers. You also notice that young professionals who ask the hard, self-reflective questions Nathan poses in *Stand Out!* accelerate their personal and career development by leaps and bounds. If growth is what you're looking for, this book is for you!"

– BOB TIEDE
Author of *Great Leaders ASK Questions* & Blogger
@LeadingWithQuestions.com

"Nathan Magnuson correctly states in his opening chapter that, *"Young professionals today are the leaders of tomorrow."* His latest book *Stand Out!* demonstrates not only that he cares about developing the next generation of leaders, but also understands the highs and lows of the journey toward becoming a leader. He skillfully, passionately, and winsomely equips and empowers young professionals. Enhanced by personal experiences, readers will find themselves encouraged in their own leadership journey and will be better for it."

– DR. DORIS GOMEZ
Dean, Regent University School of Business & Leadership

"Young professionals everywhere want to know: Is it possible to love my job and make a difference? In a business world that sometimes seems faceless and harsh, *Stand Out!* offers quick, practical, and insightful advice to help you earn respect and find meaning in your work."

– DR. JEFF MYERS
President, Summit Ministries

"You wouldn't think of going on a road trip without your GPS app handy. Neither should you set out on your career journey without a trustworthy guide. *Stand Out!* is just that. Packed with practical, actionable advice, this is the handbook for setting professional habits that will propel you to success in any field you choose. Read it, live it, share it and repeat!"

– L. DAVID KINGSLEY
Chief People Officer, Vlocity

Stand Out!

Become a Young Professional Who Wins at Work and Life

Nathan Magnuson

Softpress Publishing

Please submit permission requests to the address below:
www.nathanmagnuson.com/contact

Ordering Information
Special discounts are available on quantity purchases by corporations, associations and others. For details, please use the contact address listed above.
Books and resources referenced may include affiliate links.

Cover design: Nick Lee
Book design: William Parker

Softpress Publishing
4118 Hickory Crossroads Road
Kenly, NC 27542

ISBN-10: 1-7322744-5-2
ISBN-13: 978-1-7322744-5-7

First Edition: June 2020

For Mark Miller

Your example as a leadership development executive and author has inspired me my entire young professional career as I've attempted to trace similar footsteps. Standing on your shoulders has enabled me to see farther. I hope this book makes you proud.

Contents

Introduction

Hi, I'm Nathan. I wrote this book because I care about you.

But you don't even know me, you may be thinking. You're probably right, but let me explain.

During my final round of interviews for a past job opportunity, my prospective new bosses were impressed with my knowledge and experience but wanted a bit more convincing of my relationship-building skills. They were both big-time "people people" and didn't want to make a hiring mistake. They asked me how I demonstrated compassion at work. It was a fair question. I answered honestly that when there was a problem, I didn't tend to be the first person to give people hugs – although I could if I needed to. But I took great pride in identifying the source of the problem and solving it for good. That way, it couldn't ruin people's day anymore! That must have convinced them because they extended an offer and we worked together for several years.

If you're a young professional, we've shared some similar experiences. I know many of the challenges you've faced, problems you've encountered and times when you just needed a friend to help you cope. I've been there too. I recognize some of the scenes from your highlight reel as well. I wish I'd had a guide ready for me when I began my journey. It would've helped me cast a bigger vision while also setting more realistic expectations. It would've saved many tough lessons along the way. It would've saved a lot of time and money too. That's what I hope this book can be for you. There were definitely times when I wanted to sleep in a bit longer or watch more football games than to keep writing. But when I remembered the times when nothing seemed to make sense, I knew I had to share these encouraging words with you.

What has your young professional experience been so far?

When I reflect on the moments that have shaped my young professional experience to this point, certain ones stand out above the others, for a wide variety of reasons.

Some moments profoundly shaped who I've become, like the day in Dr. Jeff Myers' organizational leadership class when I realized I wanted to work in corporate leadership development... but had no idea how to get started. Or my first mission in Kirkuk, Iraq as a member of the U.S. Army Special Operations. Or the meeting where a senior executive decided to fire a young professional colleague for acting entitled to a promotion he hadn't earned... and I realized I'd had a similar attitude myself.

Some were really disappointing, like my 90th day in my first job after college when the thought of working in accounting for another 90 days seemed like pure torture. Or when I made it to final interviews for my dream job at my dream company after years of trying, but didn't get it. (I was so disappointed when they called to tell me that I got tongue-tied and could barely speak!) Or the day I was part of a mass layoff and told to "act professional" as security escorted me out of the building. Or the year I worked the hardest and produced the best work in my career, but my annual bonus was only 17 cents on the dollar because of the company's dismal financial performance that year.

Some were exciting, like when I was accepted into Accenture's management consulting practice and got to build a new leadership development program for the FBI. Or the day a couple senior leaders asked me how I "always knew what we should do next" and I realized for the first time I might actually have a clue what I was doing. Or the first time I asked for a big raise... and got it!

Some were just confusing, like the day I accidently wired $77 million to the wrong bank. (I'll tell you how that event impacted my career trajectory in Chapter 4.) Or the year I received an unexpected low performance review, but when I asked for specific feedback, I only received positive examples. Or the time it took 330 applications to finally land a new job.

My collection of experiences is unique to me, but I'm guessing you've been in some similar situations – situations that were inspiring, upsetting, exhilarating or disillusioning.

I'm convinced that it's more exciting to be a young professional now than at any other point in history.

Nearly everything about the way work is performed is in the midst of a major transformation. Information and analytics make it possible to "know" almost anything. Advances in technology have made almost any challenge seem possible to overcome. Communication and social media continue to shape and reshape the way we interact inside and outside of work. The rapid pace of change will remain the status quo and today's young professionals are main characters in determining the outcomes of major efforts currently underway.

Young professionals today are the leaders of tomorrow.

Young professionals today are the leaders of tomorrow.

Unfortunately, not everything about being a young professional is easy. The more options, the more hesitancy.

Are we making the right career moves? Are we missing out on something better? Why does work feel so routine? When will we land our dream job? When will our ideas be taken seriously? How can we bounce back from a major setback? Why does progress take so long? Will we ever get promoted?

If you've asked any of these questions, you're in good company. The answers are available. Not only that, your organization has a vested interest in helping you along the journey. After all, you're the one who will help them solve tomorrow's problems that they're not even aware of yet.

Let's talk for a moment about how to use this book. It's divided into ten short chapters with over fifty tips for increasing your effectiveness and engagement with your life, your work and your leadership as a young professional. We'll ask some of the deepest questions and explore some of the toughest challenges together.

Specifically, inside this book you'll learn how to:

- Take ownership in a way that makes success not just possible but probable.
- Cultivate a winning attitude that stands out among your peers.
- Articulate your personal brand and put it to productive use.
- Shape the conversation your organization is having about you in positive ways.
- Identify the key elements of a career purpose – and how to find yours.
- Find more satisfaction with the job you currently have, starting now.

- Become the team player your organization needs and will reward.
- Navigate your early career with the savvy of a seasoned veteran.
- Lead when your time comes – and even before then.
- And much more...

Remember how I said that I wrote this book because I care about you... and that I like to help solve problems? I'm a consultant at heart, so before we begin, let me share my top tips for getting the most out of this book. Use them, and it'll drastically improve your results.

- **One chapter at a time** – You could probably finish the entire book in an hour or two. Resist the urge. Read only one or two chapters at a time. You wouldn't do ten physical workouts in one day. Take the same approach with this book. You'll get much better and longer lasting results.
- **Reflect** – Each chapter includes a list of key questions to get the most from the content. Answering the questions actually has more value than reading the pages. Take the time to reflect. Journal your personal insights. Best of all, discuss them with someone else.
- **Share** – Throughout the book are short quotes, quips and tips. Share the ones that stand out to you, either on social media or with your colleagues or peer group. When you repeat an idea, it becomes your own. And don't forget to use the #youngprofessionals hashtag!
- **Enlist a buddy or small group** – No leader learns alone. You'll go farther faster when you go

partner together. Invite a group of young professional peers at work to form a book club and read along together because you can implement the ideas in the context of your organization. Or, you might pick a community or social group as well – or simply invite a buddy to join you. If you do, will you send me a note at nathan@nathanmagnuson.com and let me know how it goes?

- **Don't try to do it all** – As I mentioned, there are over 50 tips included in this book, some of which took me several years to articulate, not to mention accomplish. (And I'm still working on many of them.) You'll get overwhelmed if you try to implement all of them at the same time. For each chapter, highlight the one or two that present the greatest impact now. You can circle back to the others later on.

Legendary NFL football coach Vince Lombardi once stated, "Winning isn't everything, but the will to win is." Your time to shine is right around the corner. Are you ready to step up and stand out?

This book will help you get there.

P.S. – As a thank you for taking this journey with me, I've included a few special bonuses. The first is a list of *20 Ways to Be More (Young) Professional*. It's included at the back of the book and is also available as a separate download. It works great as a 20 day challenge for yourself or your peer group. The second is a resource called *Decision-Making Hacks for Young Professionals* to help you keep moving forward despite uncertainty. The third is called *5 Ways to Win the Hearts of Your Young Professionals*, which is geared toward leaders, executives and HR professionals. If you'd like the leaders in your organization to be more involved with young professional issues, this is the perfect resource to share with them. You can find more information about each of these bonuses waiting for you in the pages at the end of the book or by visiting www.nathanmagnuson.com/resources.

Let's get started!

1

Ownership – You're the Boss of You

If you grew up with siblings like I did, you likely had frequent arguments about who was the boss of whom. Throughout the course of the day, any given interaction was liable to escalate into a full blown confrontation, ending with someone yelling, "You're not the boss of me!" It's probably not a stretch to assume you uttered those words yourself as a youngster too.

I've come to notice that adults aren't much different than children, we just get better (sometimes) at keeping our impulses in check. But when it comes to who is boss, we'd all benefit from repeating the mantra from time to time, but with a slight variation. That's right, it'd probably do a world of good to drop what we're doing, run up to our peers, fists clenched and face puckered, and declare for the eternal record, "I'm the boss of *me*!"

> When we take ownership of our life, everything that is possible for our life expands exponentially.

Ownership. So intrusive, liberating, intimidating and empowering all at the same time. Stephen Covey identified it as "being proactive" in his first of seven habits of highly effective people.[1] John Maxwell refers to it as the Law of Intentionality.[2] Others simply call it taking personal responsibility.

Hopefully, it's not a great stretch to convince you that taking ownership of each aspect of your life is a worthy endeavor. It's a good sentiment, but what does it mean in day-to-day practice?

Accept Responsibility for Your Life Choices

Have you ever stopped to notice how many people are ready to make your choices for you, if you'll let them? Family members sometimes apply significant pressure to major life decisions. Employers have a point of view on your career trajectory. And marketers will always try to convince you that you can't live without their products – it's so obvious it shouldn't even be a choice!

Zig Ziglar observed, "You are where you are in life because of a series of choices you have made."[3] The good news is that when you change your choices, you change your outcomes. That's the liberating thing about taking ownership – it means each of us has the power to achieve greatness.

> When you change your choices, you change your outcomes.

Until you and I accept responsibility for our choices – every single one of them, past, present and future – we haven't accepted complete ownership. We're still abdicating some of the responsibility to be the "boss of me" to someone else.

Set Your Direction

Andy Stanley noted that, "Direction, not intention, determines destination." If you really are the boss of you, that means accepting the responsibility to define success on your own terms and chart your own course.

> "Direction, not intention, determines destination."
> – Andy Stanley

Self-determination sounds attractive, but it's a lot harder than it seems on the surface. It requires turning down the volume on all the other clamoring voices and opinions that are quick to intrude and choosing a route that may lead off the beaten path from time to time. And it's especially tricky for young professionals, who are still relatively new to making significant life decisions, such as what career direction (or re-direction) to pursue, where to live, how to manage their finances and whether to commit to a relationship long-term.

> You can change the course without giving up on the destination.

If you've ever felt uncomfortable making big decisions without having all the information or being 100% certain of the outcome, welcome to life. The decisions themselves won't get easier, but your ability to rise to the challenge will become more natural with practice. Keep in mind, you can change the course without giving up on the destination.

By the way, the second bonus at the end of this book *Decision-Making Hacks for Young Professionals* will help you navigate the complicated, murky decisions you encounter along your journey.

Embrace the Grind

Have you ever decided to sign up for a 5K race with your friends only to realize that training runs are tough, especially when you're a little (or a lot) out of shape? If you've been in that situation, you know that the only way to finish with a decent time and reach your goal is to push through the discomfort of your training runs. Which is the greater accomplishment: showing up for race day or showing up each day of the process leading up to it?

Almost nothing worth having comes without sustained effort. As they say, if it were easy, everyone would be doing it. Every day you commit to making progress and doing the difficult, lonely work is a day you achieve greatness. The only way to persevere when the going gets tough is to embrace the grind.

Every day you commit to making progress and doing the difficult, lonely work is a day you achieve greatness.

Build Your Resilience

It's a fact of life that not everything will go as planned on your journey to success. There will be hiccups, detours and disappointments along the way. You'll need to adjust your plans and your expectations more than once. You'll need to overcome your own mistakes. You'll also need to overcome the poor decisions of others that affect you, as well as the setbacks of life we all encounter.

That said, the unexpected brings good things too – even if they are packaged differently than we hoped or planned for.

How many setbacks will it take for you to give up? As long as the answer is, "at least one more," you'll make it. As the Japanese proverb encourages, "Fall down seven times, stand up eight."

Own the Outcome

My first experience with investing took place in 2005 in one of my business classes. I "invested" $500,000 in an online simulator that mirrored the open market for 10 weeks. By the end of the semester, I had earned a 60% annual return and had more money than everyone else in the class, including the professor.

My first real world experience with investing took place in 2007. Before going on a 12 month overseas deployment with the Army, I invested $20,000 I had meticulously saved from my signing bonus and boot camp earnings with a carefully selected and conservative professional advisor. You can probably guess what happened next. The market crashed in 2008 and a few months later my portfolio was worth only about $8,000. It still makes me a little sick thinking about it today.

How do you respond when you do everything the "right" way, but things turn out horribly wrong? For me, I could've blamed my advisor, blamed the economy or blamed bad timing. None of that would've changed the outcome.

In their book *Extreme Ownership*, ex-Navy SEALs Jocko Willink and Leif Babin sum up ownership to a T. "The leader must own everything in his or her world. There is no one else to blame."

When the twists and turns of life don't go our way, we have the opportunity to take a deep breath, accept and own the outcome, reassess and continue on. It's the first step toward achieving greatness.

You're the boss of you. Choose to be the best boss you can be. The key is ownership.

Sow a thought, reap an action
Sow an action, reap a habit
Sow a habit, reap a character
Sow a character, reap a destiny

— Ralph Waldo Emerson

Key Takeaways

1. Taking ownership is all about accepting responsibility.
2. When you change your choices, you change your outcomes.
3. Taking ownership requires hard work and overcoming adversity.
4. Blaming your situation on other people and circumstances is the opposite of ownership and will stunt your ability to make progress.

Discussion Questions

- What is one of the best choices you've made in your life so far? One of the worst choices?
- What choice are you wrestling with right now?
- What direction are you currently pointing toward? Are you taking life as it comes to you or pursuing something you've determined is meaningful and worthwhile?
- Where do you need to take more ownership in your life?
- What's the biggest setback you've overcome so far? What did you learn from it?

2

Mindset – Check Yourself Before You Wreck Yourself

For those who attended college, you probably survived more than a few late nights on little sleep and high doses of caffeine. It may have worked when cramming for a big exam, but sooner or later reality struck, and you crashed hard. Our bodies crave nourishment. Without it they won't produce high quality outcomes.

Simply put, you get out what you put in.

It's true with our bodies and even more so with our minds.

If you want to stand out as a young professional, your mindset will make you or break you. After all, it's hard to win without a winning attitude.

> It's hard to win without a winning attitude.

One of the tough realities of being a young professional is that many seasoned veterans already have you pegged. They've encountered young professionals before with a poor mindset. Fair or not, bias can run deep. It's up to you to set a new tone – for them, but even more so for yourself.

So, which mindsets are the right ones? I'd suggest starting with these.

Eschew Entitlement

When was the last time you used the word, "eschew" in a sentence? It's not a word young professionals throw around much these days – except maybe when they sneeze! But when it comes to entitlement, it's exactly the approach you need to take. The young professional generations have been plagued with the perception of narcissism for years now.[4] Justified or not, entitlement will wreck you quicker than any other mindset out there. Here's why: other people can smell it from miles away – and it stinks!

Entitlement basically says, "I deserve it before I've earned it." Even if that "something" is the result of misaligned or miscommunicated expectations, your seasoned colleagues won't put up with it for long, particularly the ones who grew up with defined career paths that rewarded hard work and loyalty over an extended period of time without the benefit of smart technology at their fingertips.

My career observations have confirmed many times over that the quickest way to sabotage both your present and future opportunities is to be seduced by entitlement. Treat it like the poison it is and work hard to smell it on yourself before anyone else does – even if it provokes a sneeze.

The New OCD: Obsessive Comparison Disorder

If there's one obstacle to developing a winning attitude that has created a whole new challenge for young professionals, it's the comparison trap – that is, the temptation to compare our experiences, accomplishments, possessions, social standing and even appearance with others. Generations expert Paul Angone calls this mentality "obsessive comparison disorder," describing it as "the compulsion to constantly compare ourselves with others, producing unwanted thoughts and feelings that drive us to depression, consumption, anxiety and all around joyous discontent."[5] Social media makes this reality all but impossible to ignore. Maybe it just comes naturally, but it's a slippery slope for our fragile psyches.

Why is OCD so demoralizing? There are really only two outcomes of playing the comparison game: feeling superior or feeling inferior. We end up arrogant or envious. Either way, we lose!

What's the solution? Celebrate the successes of others but don't use them as your own measuring stick. Find people you respect and work to follow their example, but resist the urge to play the comparison game. We're all on different stages of our own individual journeys. Your first try will never compare to others' best work. Simply focus on your next step – that's all you can do. And if you need a break from social media to get there, take it.

Your first try will never measure up to others' best work.

Beware the "As-Soon-As" Myth

Fill in these two blanks: "As soon as ______, I'll be ______."

For example: "As soon as I get that promotion, I'll be satisfied."

Circumstantial satisfaction is short-lived and unsustainable.

Forget about it. Famed actor and comedian Jim Carrey admitted as much when he observed, "I think everybody should get rich and famous and do everything they ever dreamed of so they can see it's not the answer."[6] Don't get me (or Carrey) wrong, good things are good. But if you can't be satisfied without them, you'll never be satisfied with them. The new becomes normal almost before you can blink. Circumstantial satisfaction is short-lived and unsustainable.

Grateful Heart, Happy Heart

I'm convinced that wherever you are in life, there is always someone more qualified than you who would work harder at your job for less money than you're currently making. That shouldn't make you feel guilty or defensive, but it should make you think twice about the things you complain about. Each of us is truly blessed. Why don't we acknowledge it, much less act like it?

When was the last time you took inventory of your blessings? Have you ever made a gratitude list?

Dale Carnegie advised to, "Count your blessings, not your sorrows."

King Solomon observed, "To the happy heart, life is a continual feast."

And Abraham Lincoln noted, "Most people are about as happy as they make up their minds to be."

Be grateful and you'll be the happy one of the bunch. Happy young professionals are hard not to notice for all the best reasons. Don't wait until later to be happy. Gratitude is your greatest ally.

Don't wait until later to be happy. Gratitude is your greatest ally.

Stay Humble & Hungry

In his book, *The Ideal Team Player*, Patrick Lencioni describes the type of people to recruit for your dream team as hungry, humble and smart.[7] This book will help you with the smart part, but let's talk a moment about humble and hungry.

Humble young professionals don't think less of themselves, they just think of themselves less. They work toward the success of others. They possess the confidence and character to willingly share the spotlight. We'll discuss this more in Chapter 8.

Hungry young professionals can't wait to get to work! They accept ownership and focus on delivering great results while embracing the grind today. They know that hard work eventually gets rewarded.

You don't need humility at the expense of hunger. Like pepperoni on a pizza, they go best together. Humility without hunger is apathetic. Hunger without humility is reckless.

Humility without hunger is apathetic. Hunger without humility is reckless.

Zig Ziglar famously stated, "You are what you are and where you are because of what has gone into your mind. You can change what you are and where you are by changing what goes into your mind."[8]

Your mindset determines your destiny.

You can possess all the talent in the world, but it's your mindset that determines your destiny.

Key Takeaways

1. It's hard to win without a winning attitude.
2. Entitlement will sabotage you almost immediately.
3. When you compare yourself with others, you'll feel dissatisfied with what you have and who you are.
4. Don't wait until later to be happy. Gratitude is your greatest ally.
5. Hunger and humility are an unstoppable combination.
6. Your mindset determines your destiny.

Discussion Questions

- When has entitlement gotten the better of you in the past? Where do you need to watch out for it in the present?
- Who can you emulate as a positive example of what you aspire to become?
- Who should you avoid comparing yourself with to protect your sense of accomplishment and self-worth?
- How grateful of person would others describe you as? (Tip: Take the 100x gratitude challenge – sit down and don't get up until you've recorded 100 things you're grateful for!)
- Where do you need to be more humble? More hungry?

3

Identity – Know Thyself

In the romantic comedy movie *Hitch*, Kevin James' character Albert Brennen resists dating consultant Alex Hitchens' advice to wear a particularly classy outfit to a special night out. "I'm just not sure these shoes are *me*," he protests.

Hitch, played by Will Smith, responds, "Right now, 'You' is a very fluid concept." He then goes on to describe the look, attitude and vibe Albert should portray to pull off a successful date. Predictably, the date goes horribly wrong and it's not until Albert starts acting like himself that things turn around for the better.

Identity is one of the key questions defining young professional culture today. "*Who am I?*" we silently wonder.

Like Hitch, your peers, colleagues, advertisers and society as a whole are quick to answer the question, "Who *should* I be?" But understanding the inner DNA of your true identity requires an intentional and extensive discovery process that only you can initiate. It won't just define your present but will determine what you hope to become in the future as well.

Identity can't be outsourced.

Identity can't be outsourced.

So how can you begin to answer the identity question in a way that positively influences personal and professional outcomes? Self-awareness is a process, and these areas are a great place to start.

Passion

"Follow your passion." It's a sentiment that gets thrown around often in inspirational speeches, friendly advice and social media posts. Intuitively, we know we ought to pay attention, but the competing instinct of sensibility disguised as maturity threatens passion in its tracks. Chip Heath and Dan Heath refer to it as the "soul-sucking force of reasonableness."

But passion doesn't care about reason. Do you know why? Passion comes from the heart, not the head. It's meant to be explored, not ignored.

Passion comes from the heart, not the head. It's meant to be explored, not ignored.

In an iconic commencement speech in 2014, Jim Carrey shared a lesson learned from observing the career choices of his father. "So many of us choose our path out of fear disguised as practicality. What we really want seems impossibly out of reach and ridiculous to expect... I learned many great lessons from my father, not the least of which is that you can fail at what you don't want. So you might as well take a chance on doing what you love."[9]

The goal for every passion shouldn't be a full-time career opportunity. (Otherwise we'd be forced to limit the things we're passionate about.) But neither is contemplating our areas of passion a form of immaturity. Passion is a gift that can and should help inform both our career and involvement decisions.

If identifying areas of passion is difficult for you, consider some of the following questions:

- What excites you?
- What are you intensely interested in?
- What activities cause you to lose track of time?
- What could you talk about for hours?
- What do you lose sleep over, for better *and* worse?

The bottom line is that it's hard to make a difference doing something we're not passionate about. Lean into your areas of passion, not away, because passion is connected to your identity.

Strengths

What's the difference between a superhero who hasn't discovered his superpower yet and an average Joe? Not much, aside from an awkward encounter here and there.

You may not possess superpowers, but each of us has a unique combination of innate strengths at our disposal, provided we take the time to identify and harness them. Some of us are natural communicators. Others are natural planners or organizers or relationship-builders. Operating in our strengths allows us to produce work that, as Gallup states, "consistently provides near-perfect performance."[10] Just like superpowers, unidentified strengths are impotent. After all, it's hard to play to your strengths when you don't know what your strengths are.

It's hard to play to your strengths when you don't know what your strengths are.

There are many ways to discover your strengths, but the easiest one I've found is to join the 20 million+ individuals who have taken the StrengthsFinder® assessment from Gallup.[11]

Personality Tendencies

Have you ever wondered if your personality was a blessing or a curse? I have more than once. I've finally realized that when it comes to our personality tendencies, like strengths, knowledge is power. What we don't know can't help us, but it can definitely hurt us.

Right out of college, I assumed that personality mostly boiled down to whether you were an introvert or an extrovert. I'm an introvert, so I picked a job in accounting that wouldn't require significant levels of interaction. It was a huge mistake. It wasn't until later on that I discovered my preference for relying on intuition in making decisions and solving problems collaboratively and creatively, which is usually frowned upon in accounting!

If you've ever wondered why some people don't "get" you, it's possible that you don't quite get yourself.

Fortunately there are tools available to help you discover your personality tendencies. Invest time taking a Myers-Briggs Type Indicator® (MTBI®) or DiSC® assessment and read through your personality profile report. "You" are much more than your assortment of traits, but the insights can provide immediate benefits in terms of actionable self-knowledge.

> If you've ever wondered why some people don't "get" you, it's possible that part of the dynamic is that you don't quite get yourself.

Blind Spots

Have you ever had the misfortune of being told by someone else that they "know you better than you know yourself?" It's not a very empathetic statement, but there is usually at least a partial ring of truth to it.

One of the tricky parts about being a young professional is that our own self-awareness is limited by our relatively short life and career experience. This means others can notice aspects of our behavior we're still blind to – words or phrases we use, mannerisms and body language that can have unintended effects on others or patterns in our logical processes. Sometimes they're right about us and sometimes they're not. Either way, it's a beneficial wealth of knowledge if we're humble enough to seek the insights of those around us, or at least consider them when they're shared with us.

Personal Brand

When I was first introduced to the notion of a "personal brand," I'll admit I chafed at the concept. It sounded egotistical and self-centered. But one day a seemingly random experience convinced me otherwise.

As I was walking to lunch in downtown Dallas, a car swerved right in front of me in the crosswalk. I did what most reasonable people would do, throwing up my hands angrily and shooting a nasty look. But as I continued on my way, I wondered if any of my coworkers had seen me. Since part of my job was to develop and deliver leadership training, I considered how my antics on the street might affect my credibility in the training room. I decided that if I were them watching me, I'd think less of me after that outburst. I decided I needed to exercise greater self-control.

> A personal brand is simply the experience you want others to have with you.

A personal brand is simply the experience you want others to have with you.

When it comes to my own personal brand, I want to be perceived as knowledgeable and credible, but also positive, mature and encouraging. In that moment on the crosswalk, I decided that spontaneous outbursts, even when justified, didn't fit that identity. Not only that, all brands require consistency in order to build trust.

It's easy to feel anonymous sometimes, but I can tell you from experience that it's almost never the case – especially in our workplaces. In most situations, our reputation precedes and exceeds us. We can't control the conversation about us that is already taking place, but we can influence it. The first step is to determine what experience we want others to have with us, like I did after nearly getting hit by the impatient driver. The second is to curb our behavior in that direction.

> Age is a high price to pay for maturity.

Identity is a lifelong discovery process with twists and turns as we continue to learn and grow. If we keep asking the question, "Who am I, *really*?" we should expect to know ourselves better at age 80 than we do at age 70, and at age 23 than at age 22. Just keep in mind that age is a high price to pay for maturity. Just because we grow older doesn't guarantee we become more self-aware. It's intentionality that makes the difference. Like all forms of growth, the destination is worth the journey.

Key Takeaways

1. Identity can't be outsourced. Be who you are to the fullest extent.
2. If you don't understand yourself, it's unrealistic to expect other people to understand you.
3. It's hard to play to your strengths when you don't know what your strengths are.
4. The younger and more inexperienced you are, the more blind spots you'll have.
5. Be intentional about determining the experience you want other people to have with you – your personal brand.

Discussion Questions

- What are you passionate about? How can you increase your involvement in your areas of passion?
- What are a couple strengths you know you possess – areas where you can produce quality outcomes without much effort?
- Do those same strengths ever get you into trouble? How so?
- Have you ever been misguided about your own personality tendencies in the past? What happened as a result and what set you straight?
- When was the last time you became aware of one of your blind spots? What happened and what did you do with the new insight?
- What experience do you want other people to have with you?

4

Clarity – You Can't Have a Successful Career if You Don't Know What You Want

I sat staring blankly at the computer screen in my cubicle. I'd been lucky enough to find my first job five weeks after graduating from college. It was an accounting role in a commercial lending department at a national bank division in Kansas City. I wasn't getting paid much, but I'd been able to buy a cheap car and could afford to pay my landlords (parents) rent for occupying their basement. At the very least, I was moving in the right direction of responsible adulthood.

But I hated it. Oh, did I hate it.

I had just completed my 90-day probation period – meaning that I was now an official employee. But the thought of being there another 90 days made my stomach churn.

Just a few months earlier I'd been alternating between pick-up tennis matches with "the fellas" by day and Rook card games by night. Even though my classmates called me a robot for my dedication to my schoolwork, I still managed to have plenty of good times. Every day was an adventure.

As I stared at the office wall, all I could wish for in that moment was for a mini basketball hoop to appear so I could jump up for an impromptu slam dunk and escape the quiet sounds of typing and polite sneezes.

What do you do when everything you prepared for lands you in the last place on earth you want to be? In that moment, I only had questions, but no answers.

What did I do wrong? I asked myself. *I thought I did the right thing. I did what I was "supposed" to do. I did what "they" said I should do. I did the responsible thing. I went to school and even graduated early. And then I got a job. No gap year for me, I can't afford it. Is this my life sentence? Am I going to spend the next 40+ years stuck in this cubicle, unless I die of boredom, which may happen at any moment?*

It got worse. I started getting the Sunday night blues. I was fidgety all the time. I tried to make my work take as long as possible just so my plate wouldn't be completely empty.

Then one day, I wired $77 million to the wrong bank.

I'm not even kidding. The worst part is, I didn't realize it until the vice president called me on the phone.

"Where's our money?" he asked. I told him I'd have to call him back.

The mistake actually turned out to be pretty easy to correct. A phone call and a new wire request and all was back to normal, even though I'm sure my kerfuffle was the story of the day with my supervisors.

But I couldn't take it anymore.

I just can't do this. I have too much pride to make another $77 million mistake... but deciphering all the legal documentation in these loan portfolios is killing me. I want to change the world, not generate reports and schedule *remittance wires that will all soon be automated to work without me. I want to make things happen!*

But what else should I do? If I look for another job, how will I predict if I will like that job any more than this one? What if I actually like it less??

What is it that you want when it comes to your career?

In case you think this is only a young professional problem, consider a recent LinkedIn study which found that 90% of global professionals want to hear from recruiters about new job opportunities, whether they are casual or serious job seekers.[12] The fact that this is inclusive of all generations should be sobering to young professionals – we can't expect the answers to simply come with time.

The problem isn't simply a lack of engagement (although we'll talk about that in Chapter 7). After spending all of childhood and adolescence being asked what we want to be when we grow up, our unsubstantiated expectations are ripe for disappointment. Even worse, when we realize there are far more possibilities than we first assumed, evaluating the options can be downright paralyzing!

My turmoil in my first job after college didn't have anything to do with the organization. It was a strong company but the job in accounting was a poor fit for me. I was miserable. The problem was, I didn't know why. It's easy to react to what we don't like but difficult to know what we really want. I wasn't able to move forward until I could articulate what I wanted in a career – a process that required a few years of intense soul searching and continues to be an important aspect of

> It's easy to react to what we don't like but difficult to know what we really want.

my self-evaluation process. As my friend Scott Wozniak once posted on social media, "If you don't know the life you want, you can't run toward it. If you don't run toward what you want, it won't happen for you. A meaningful life is a choice."

To complicate matters even further, many of us grew up hearing the well-meaning message, "You can be anything you want to be. Don't settle for less!" Nothing like a strong dose of FOMO to add more pressure!

So how do you determine what you want from a career after a lifetime of hearing that you can be anything you want to be? The answer lies less in what's "out there" and more in what's inside of us.

Here are eight core questions that can help bring career clarity – questions that took significant time for me to answer, but turned out to make all the difference in the career moves that I made since my days of misplaced $77 million wire transfers.

What past experiences have provided the highest sense of pride and accomplishment?

Sometimes the biggest clues to our success and engagement in the future lie in our past. We've all had experiences we found particularly rewarding over the course of our life. Treat these experiences like unmined gold. It's time to start digging.

> Sometimes the biggest clues to our success and happiness are in the past rather than the future.

I once worked with a career coach who advised me to record as many meaningful accomplishments that I could think of in my life up to that point – and the earlier in life they took place, the better. He said to pay special attention to my role in the accomplishment and include the part that gave me the highest degree of satisfaction. Then we looked for common themes together. Some of my best memories were creating coded football plays with my brother to beat the neighborhood kids in the backyard, learning to juggle (and making it into a business) and leading a major research project in college. The themes included the autonomy to create my own goals, setting the strategy and delivering the outcomes in a public forum – and sometimes competitively. My coach encouraged me to pursue similar themes as an adult in my career. If I did, I'd replicate the sense of accomplishment I felt in those experiences growing up.

It's uncanny how accurate that assessment of past experiences continues to be for me even now, over a decade later. It's gotten to the point that I can predict whether I'll enjoy or despise a potential job opportunity – and then make my career decisions accordingly.

Your past may be the key to your future as well. At the very least, it holds powerful clues. Don't settle for random career choices when you have the benefit of past life experiences that can help guide you toward success and personal satisfaction.

What interests do you want to pursue?

What do you do in your spare time? Some people catalogue insects by species. Others watch old television shows and evaluate set designs. I have a friend who photographs LEGO people in public settings. Sometimes I'll go on a leadership book reading binge and wonder why anyone *wouldn't* want to spend their weekend that way.

Not all hobbies should become career pursuits, but our interests should inform our aspirations. After all, there are professionals who study insects, design TV show sets and write leadership books. Why shouldn't you be one of them? If you have strong interests, don't ignore them; explore them. It's never been easier to create a career opportunity from your interests than it is today. And if you are completely uninterested in what you do, it's past time to make a change.

It's never been easier to create a career opportunity from your interests than it is today.

What types of problems do you most like to solve?

Whenever I have the chance to interview or banter with colleagues in my field of corporate leadership development, I always ask, "Which part of our field do you enjoy the most?"

Usually they say they enjoy the "ah-ha" look on people's faces when facilitating a leadership session. The problem they enjoy solving is a lack of knowledge or awareness and the solution is teaching new concepts. For me the answer is much different. I'm a consultant first, so my favorite moment is when I get the "ah-ha" of figuring out how to solve a complicated problem when I'm by myself in front of a whiteboard or PowerPoint slide and then coming up with a solution to present to an executive team. I enjoy being able to "see" the solution far in advance.

Consider these contrasting types of problems. For each contrast, see if you can identify which ones you enjoy solving the most.

- Routine/common problems
- Rare problems

• Simple problems	• Complex problems
• People problems	• Process problems
• Many problems at once	• One problem at a time
• Small-scale problems	• Large-scale problems
• Limited scope of problems (as a specialist)	• Broad scope of problems (as a generalist)
• Spontaneous problems	• Strategic problems
• Problems that must be solved immediately	• Problems that require time to understand and solve
• Solving problems as an individual	• Solving problems as a team

As you can tell, there is great diversity in types of problems, problem-solving processes and solutions. The closer you come to identifying your preferred types, the easier it is to seek out your ideal problem-solving environments.

What role do you like to play?

The more work experiences I gain, the more I become convinced that picking the right "role to perform" is as or more important that choosing the ideal field. Unfortunately, that notion flies in the face of most career advice we receive growing up or the way educational and corporate development programs are designed. If you take a football kicker and try to make him into a linebacker, isn't it reasonable to expect he'll lose interest in the sport and start thinking about playing soccer instead?

The individual positions we take matter, but so does the nature of the role *on the team*. For instance, here is just a sample of the many different types of roles people play in nearly any field:

- Advisor
- Agent
- Auditor
- Boss
- Buyer
- Coach
- Encourager
- Energizer
- Executor
- Expert
- Facilitator
- Fixer
- Interpreter
- Liaison
- Negotiator
- Presenter
- Project manager
- Promoter
- Relationship-builder
- Researcher
- Seller
- Trainer

A good way to think about the role you naturally like to play is to finish the sentence, "I like to be the go-to person others rely on when they need someone who can ________."

What *don't* you want to do?

There are too many career options to pick a direction solely based on the process of elimination. It would take many lifetimes! That said, what we know that we *don't* want can provide strong guiding clarity for our career decisions, even when we aren't quite sure of the way forward.

On my year-long overseas deployment with the military, I noticed the extra degree of difficulty experienced by my battle buddies with spouses and children back home. I decided I did not want a job where I would be absent from loved ones for months at a time. As a big box consultant, I realized I was likely to be staffed on projects outside my area of interests and expertise from time to time. I decided I did not want my work to be dependent on the whims of clients with changing priorities and ultimately left to join a corporate team.

Just as it takes experience to refine our interests, it also takes experience to inform our "don't want" list. They emerge as we progress, if we pay attention.

Where do you want to live?

As a teenager, my Uncle Ted remarked to me that if you enjoy a particular city, you can move there for a year or two just because you want to. The thought intimidated me at the time. But as fate would have it, I ended up living in many more cities as a young professional than I had originally planned.

Uncle Ted's comment turned out to be futuristic not just for me, but for my generation. One growing trend currently befuddling employers is that today's young professionals often move to their desired destination city and then find a job there – instead of moving after they attain a job.[13] That's quite a shift from past generations.

If you haven't considered where you'd like to live, give it some serious thought. Do you like big cities or small towns? Mountains or beaches? Warm weather or cold? Different local economies support different industries as well, such as technology, energy, financial services, healthcare, insurance, media, performance arts, etc., which can further broaden your options.

What environments do you enjoy most?

The environments you occupy will shape you. They aren't created equal. It's important to pick ones where you can thrive. As an example, a nurse working in an adrenaline-inducing emergency room setting may share an

> The environments you occupy will shape you.

environment more similar to a Wall Street trading floor than the hospice care unit in the same facility.

Do you prefer environments characterized by peace and quiet? Chaos? Quick pace? Slower pace? Relationship-oriented? Results-driven?

Whenever you interview for a new job, one of the questions you ought to ask is, "What kind of person succeeds here?" This will give you insight into the corporate culture, but it's up to you to determine which type of environment you're looking for to begin with.

What are your personal values?

Core values have gotten a lot of attention in recent years in terms of corporate marketing. We all know we ought to value respect, integrity, service and excellence. But here I'm talking about your personal values – the ones you can use to practically guide your choices about work and life.

For instance, do you value travel? Physical fitness? Collaboration? Constantly learning new things? Time spent outdoors? Time spent indoors? Which elements must be present for you to feel happy and fulfilled?

At one point I tried hard to recruit my friend Josh Erickson to move to North Texas. He refused, citing the lack of mountains and instead moved to Montana to work at a luxury outdoor ranch. Josh's LinkedIn profile clearly shares some of his personal values: "I believe in travel, great customer service, quality marketing and am passionate about helping people explore the world." That's a high degree of values-awareness.

One of my closely held personal values is autonomy – the ability to determine and execute what I believe is the right course of action and also to set my own calendar, as much as possible. This plays a huge factor in whether or not I'm happy and engaged with my work, colleagues and organization.

Other people can't dictate your personal values for you. It's up to you to spend the time identifying the most meaningful ones for yourself. You'll be the one who gains the most.

Other people can't dictate your personal values for you.

Choosing an ideal career goes much deeper than simply picking between job opportunities. After all, as young professionals, our careers are more likely to contain a portfolio of experiences than a defined career path when it's all said and done. We all gain clarity over time – that's part of the discovery process. But you do yourself a great favor by asking the tough questions as early as possible.

So how did I escape the accounting gig? I wish I had had this book to guide me – it would've saved a lot of time, money and grief! I ended up working in the accounting job for two years, even though I knew immediately it was a poor fit. But halfway through, I enlisted in the Army Reserves, which allowed me to pay off my student loans and begin graduate school to explore a career change. Shortly afterward, I spent 12 months on a deployment to Iraq. When I returned, I finished graduate school and was fortunate enough to secure a position with Accenture's management consulting practice. From there, I've enjoyed several staff and consulting roles in corporate leadership development.

If I had to do it all over again, I would've made some different decisions – as would most people. But each new opportunity was a chance to learn and grow, which informed my next steps. Even though I work in a field that fulfills me, I regularly use all the criteria in this chapter to continually evaluate my fit, effectiveness and future goals.

What is it you want in a career? It's a more complicated question than it appears on the surface. Answer it well, and you'll quicken your pace to significance.

I'd rather make a living just being myself
Than a killing being someone else

— Steve Moakler, Rather Make a Living

Key Takeaways

1. It's easy to react to what we don't like, but difficult to know what we really want.
2. Our past experiences provide enormous clues into what we'll find meaningful in the future.
3. Don't ignore your interests, let them guide you.
4. There are many different types of problems that need solving and we all gravitate to our own preferred mix.
5. The role you play on a team can be as important as the work that you do.
6. Your environments will shape you, so choose them wisely.
7. Visit and re-visit your personal values and incorporate them into your career decision-making process.

Discussion Questions

- What is one accomplishment before the age of 18 that provided you with a great sense of pride? Before the age of 12? What role did you play and what about it are you most proud of? What are the common themes?
- What interests do you lose track of time exploring?
- What types of problems do you like to solve?
- What type of role do you enjoy performing?
- Where are three places you'd find interesting to live?
- What types of environments do you speculate would fit you best?
- What are three personal values you hold deeply?

5

Discovery – 10 Myths of Finding Your "Dream Job"

Recently I attended a reception in Dallas with The Halftime Institute – an organization that helps successful professionals (usually executives in their forties and fifties) identify their sense of purpose and re-launch the second half of their careers in a more personally fulfilling direction. I couldn't help but comment to the older attendees that we young professionals don't need an institute to tell us to look for significance in our work. It's built into our generational DNA from the start! We're headed in the right direction, but unfortunately, there are a lot of unrealistic expectations among young professionals when it comes to our pursuit of meaningful work.

You may have heard it said, "Find a job you love, and you'll never work a day in your life." Maybe you've even repeated that mantra yourself a time or two. It's inspiring, encouraging and... unfortunately pretty inaccurate.

All legal and ethical work has intrinsic purpose, but it's called "work" for a reason. There will always be difficulties, challenges and occasional disappointments along the way, if for no other reason than because humans are flawed creatures. Given enough time, we'll eventually let each other down a time or two.

That said, the reason it's important to find work you love is because the passion and energy it creates will allow you to rise above the challenges.

> It's important to find work you love because the passion and energy it creates will allow you to rise above the challenges.

I'm not quite sure where the notion of a "dream job" came from, but in young professional circles, it's a borderline obsession. "What's your dream job?" we're asked. And if we can't respond, we wonder if something is broken inside of us. After all, who wants to settle for just a plain old regular job?

The damage of dream job thinking isn't the notion of dream jobs themselves, but the myths we pick up about them along the way. These myths have the power to frustrate and sabotage our aspirations for our future. On the other hand, the truth will set us free.

Let's take a look at some of the most prominent dream job myths.

Myth #1: I can be anything I want to be.

Unlike the past, this generation of young professionals has grown up being told they can be and have whatever they want in life. It's gotten so extreme that Millennials have earned the title Generation Me.[14] Of course, this positive affirmation is much better than the alternative. But when things don't work out as planned, many young professionals become disillusioned by unrealized expectations. In some cases they're stuck with expensive student loans while picking up the pieces of a failed career opportunity. In others, they simply feel stuck trying to figure out where things went wrong. It's hard to tell which is worse: the sense of disappointment or betrayal.

It's a basic fact of life that none of us can be *anything* we want to be simply because there are things in life we can't control.

At a bulky 7'1, Shaquille O'Neal would make a terrible race horse jockey.

At a slim 5'3, Prince wouldn't have stood a chance as a sumo wrestler.

But what they did choose to do and be was pretty special.

Personal limitations, while disappointing, can actually clarify and accelerate our path to a better, brighter future, including at work.

You can be *almost* anything you want to be... and probably more of it than you think. The key is to do the hard work of determining what you want and what you have to contribute.

Truth: You can't be anything you want, but you can be something incredibly special.

Myth #2: There is one perfect job out there for me.

One of the biggest mistakes we make when considering dream jobs, or any desired future, is singularity bias. We think there is only one soulmate, one ideal future and one dream job out there for us.

There are two big problems with this train of thought. First, if things don't go our way, that means we're forever relegated to a consolation life. What a bummer! Second, it's based on a fixed mindset rather than a growth mindset. A fixed

A growth mindset says there are many options if we have the discipline and creativity to find them.

mindset says there is only one ideal path forward. A growth mindset says there are many options if we have the discipline and creativity to find them.

I like how author and career expert Dan Miller describes following a purpose-filled career. He says it's like picking the right cruise ship. But on the ship there are hundreds of rooms and you get to pick which one you want to have – and you have the ability to change rooms many times and still arrive at your destination.

Be less worried about missing out on your ideal dream job and more focused on putting your passion, interests and strengths to productive use. Why settle for one dream job when you could have many of them?

Truth: There are many jobs that can satisfy what matters most to you.

Myth #3: What I was "meant" to do will never change.

As a three year-old, my dream job was to be a garbage man, jumping on and off the back of a moving truck. When I was twelve, I couldn't imagine anything better than being an NFL quarterback. I believe I've found a career field that fits me better than either of those two options, but my passions and interests continue to expand.

Johann Wolfgang von Goethe famously said, "Dream no small dreams, for they stir not the hearts of men."

Our first problem isn't that we dream too big, but that we dream too small. Our second problem is that we hang onto our dreams even after we've outgrown them.

When we dream big and move in that direction, our options expand. There are always bigger possibilities over each new horizon.

Our first problem isn't that we dream too big, but that we dream too small. Our second problem is that we hang onto our dreams even after we've outgrown them.

Truth: Both your dreams and your opportunities will change over time as you and your environments expand.

Myth #4: My "dream job" will find me.

In his book *The Rules of the Red Rubber Ball*, author and inspirational speaker Kevin Carroll tells of his passion for athletics, which began as a young boy on the playground. His pursuit of sports provided him roles as an athlete, trainer, coach and public figure. Each step of the way, he had to do what he called "the lonely work." Recalling his time learning to become an athletic trainer, Carroll noted that he probably taped the ankles of every kid in the neighborhood.[15] It took several different jobs that required discipline, hustle and persistence before others took notice. Eventually, more exciting opportunities began to seek him.

Jack London said, "You can't wait for inspiration. You have to go after it with a club."

The world won't stop to notice where you are on your dream job journey. It's up to you to join the chase.

Truth: You'll need to do the hard work of seeking or creating your meaningful career opportunities.

Myth #5: I'll recognize my dream job when I see it.

One of my favorite questions to ask young children is what they want to be when they grow up. (Pressure free, of course!) It's fascinating to see their cognitive processes develop. They want to be artists and doctors and princesses. (And in one case, a fire truck!) But as you know, most potential opportunities are invisible to their imaginations simply because they haven't encountered the issues many career fields work to solve. A child may demonstrate an aptitude for math early on, but she likely won't understand the field of corporate financial auditing until much later.

Zig Ziglar said, "Most people don't know what they want because they don't know what is available for them."

When we begin our careers, we still lack context. We don't know what all is available for us. We can read books (like this one) and ask lots of questions, but it's our experiences that inform us the most.

Do a job, considered which parts you like best, try to incorporate more of them the next time and repeat. After a few iterations, don't be surprised if a dream job emerges.

Truth: A dream job is more likely to be revealed along the way than upfront.

Myth #6: My dream job is available right now.

As a kid, my brother Cale dreamed of being a military fighter pilot. His first model airplane was an F-18 Hornet. As a teenager and young adult, Cale pursued other interests before deciding at age 25 to apply to the U.S. Marine Corps flight program. Here's what happened:

- It took one year to be selected into the program.
- It took three months to begin initial training.
- It took nine months to complete Officer Candidate School and the Basic Officer Course.
- It took a year and a half to complete ground school and primary flight training.
- It took three months to recover from a personal injury.
- It took an additional three months to overcome a training delay caused by another student pilot's error.
- It took almost two years to complete tactical jet training, after the unplanned delays.
- It took over a year to qualify to fly the Harrier and report to his unit.

In all, it took Captain Cale "Rowdy" Magnuson almost seven years from the time he applied to the flight program until he was able to report for duty as a Harrier pilot. In fact, only a handful of pilots qualify to fly the Harrier in any given year.

How many things have you wanted for seven years?

In his book *Quitter*, Jon Acuff writes an incredible chapter titled "Falling in Like with a Job You Don't Love." I really appreciate what he has to say about the process of pursuing a dream job. "Every dream takes longer than you want it to. Our time frame is always shorter and faster than what a dream has in mind. And if we rush it, if we don't give it time to incubate, we usually end up killing it before it even has a chance to breathe."[16]

If you want a chance at a dream job, you've got to be willing to play the long game. In many cases, what you want won't be available until you've completed a series of preparatory steps along the way.

If you want a chance at a dream job, you've got to be willing to play the long game.

Truth: Your dream job will likely require more time and hard work than you think.

Myth #7: I'll never have to sacrifice to attain my dream job.

I don't know why this myth exists, to be honest with you. I expect it's a combination of naiveté, misguided expectations and perhaps a dose of unconfronted entitlement. Anything worth having requires a degree of give and take. For instance, if we want to live downtown, we might sacrifice by living with a roommate or driving a cheap car. We might work an additional part-time job for a while to build new skills or to reach a financial goal. For those with a college degree, isn't spending four years and tens of thousands of dollars a sacrifice? Why should we expect a dream job to be any different?

This isn't a book about financial stewardship, but many dreams (dream jobs included) have a financial component to them. Many small business ventures require startup capital, for instance – and almost all take time to generate sufficient cash flow.

What I'm trying to say is that if your finances aren't in order, you'll have to forgo the opportunity to chase a dream job that might otherwise be within reach. Or the pursuit will take longer than necessary. Live within your means. Avoid debt like the plague. Put some money away so it's available to invest toward a dream job that presents itself. And expect to hustle extra when a dream job is in reach.

Truth: All dreams (including dream jobs) require a degree of sacrifice.

Myth #8: I can attain my dream job if I just execute my plan.

What do you do when life presents you with a better opportunity than the one you've had your heart set on? Have you ever faced a decision to let go of your carefully crafted plan in order to pursue something exciting that came out of the blue?

At some point, we've all got to recognize that life has an irrational, confounding and uncontrollable element of serendipity. As a very strategic and focused person, even writing this section drives me a little crazy! In fact, this entire book is meant as a guide to thoughtfully identify and achieve success – *on your terms*. We understand that life sometimes hands us lemons. But what are we supposed to think when we're busy trying to make lemonade and then life returns with a milkshake instead?

While living in Atlanta, I received a job offer to take what at the time represented a dream job. There was only one problem: it was located in Washington, D.C. I didn't want to move to D.C., but they wouldn't budge. I went dragging my feet. Turns out, it was the best thing that could've happened for me, professionally, socially and spiritually. I was given the opportunity to help build a leadership development program from scratch at the FBI. You can't pay for that type of experience! Even the challenges I faced and mistakes I made have recycled themselves for my benefit many times over.

My friend Daniel Jacobs once spent a few weeks volunteering with at-risk orphans in Guatemala. While there, he noticed that children who owned very little acted happier than children in the United States who seemed to have much more. So he founded a chocolate company called "Placebo Effect" with the purpose of spreading the joy he'd seen in the Guatemalan kids. The vision was right, but Daniel quickly discovered he was a terrible chocolatier. So he steered in another direction, dropping the chocolate but keeping the focus on sharing inspirational messages for personal development. From there, the company underwent several additional transformations and a name change. Today, "Avanoo" provides video-based corporate learning solutions to many Fortune 500 companies using an innovative storytelling concept. Had Daniel skipped any of the chocolate-covered lemons in the process, Avanoo wouldn't be where it is today – and neither would he. And Daniel is no stranger to embracing the unexpected – he met his wife Nathalie on an international trip when *both of them* accidently got on the wrong bus!

I don't know how to "preempt" serendipity, but I have learned it seems to show up most often when we're hard at work and actively pursuing our goals while keeping an open mind. Another analogy I use is looking for an open door. Sometimes we're so set on kicking in a closed door that we fail to notice an open one right next to it. Expect the unexpected and you'll encounter exciting new possibilities along the way.

Truth: When you expect the unexpected, you may discover a bigger dream than you initially had in mind.

Myth #9: A dream job is a destination.

Ralph Waldo Emerson observed, "A mind once stretched by a new idea, never returns to its original dimensions."

In many ways, a new dream job is similar to a new idea. It's exciting at first but the new becomes normal almost immediately. Pretty soon, we're used to it and start looking down the road again.

A meaningful career is more than just a series of jobs, it's a "path to becoming." In fact, the worst thing we can do when we land our first dream job is to settle for it. There is always more to learn and become – and after that, to do.

The worst thing we can do when we land our first dream job is to settle for it.

Truth: A dream career is a journey, not a destination.

Myth #10: Once I find my dream job, I will be happy.

I used to think that if I attained my particular dream job (at the time), I'd wake up laughing each morning. I now know that isn't true. Here's why.

If you aren't happy without a dream job, you'll never be happy with one.

Happiness and contentment are available, but they aren't dependent on a dream job. As mentioned in Chapter 2, happiness is a choice that is available to each of us, every day, regardless of our circumstances. Sure, dream jobs are desirable and should be pursued, but if you don't choose to be happy without a dream job, you'll never be happy with one.

Truth: You can choose to be happy every day, regardless of which job you have at the moment.

So how much time and emotional energy should we devote to finding our dream job?

Here's what I think: if the concept of a "dream job" inspires you, use it. Think in those terms, as long as you don't fall victim to any of the myths. On the other hand, if it confuses or frustrates you, let it go. That's okay too.

In either case, focus on maximizing your current opportunity and reaching for the next and you'll end up in a great place.

Remember, meaningful, purposeful work is available for each of us.

Key Takeaways

1. All work is challenging, that's why it's so important to find work that is meaningful to you.
2. The notion of "dream jobs" can confuse us as much as guide us.
3. You can't be anything you want to be, but you can be something incredibly special.
4. Many jobs over your working lifetime can qualify as dream jobs.
5. Dream jobs require patience, persistence and hard work.
6. You will change and grow over time, so your dream jobs should change and grow as well.

Discussion Questions

- Which dream job myth have you believed in the past? What happened to change your mindset?
- Has it been easy or difficult to know what you want to pursue next?
- Does the term "dream job" make you feel excited or stressed?
- What was your dream job as a kid? Is it still your dream job now or have you changed your mind?
- What is your dream job right now?
- How might life be presenting a new opportunity that is different from what you've planned for?
- Which dream job myth do you most need to bust at this stage of your career journey?

6

Growth – If You're Not Learning, You're Petrifying!

Soon after college, I read a statistic demonstrating that the average college graduate spends more money on coffee and soft drinks over the course of a lifetime than on personal and professional development. I vowed right there on the spot that statistic wouldn't apply to me. I can also report it's what I've learned *after* school that has made the biggest impact on my career success, rather than in the classroom.

For young professionals, this shouldn't come as a huge surprise. Past generations didn't need to learn as rapidly or extensively. If you stayed in the same job or career for decades, learning could pass as a hobby rather than a necessity. But in today's knowledge environment, obsolescence is lurking just around the corner. Since new knowledge is produced at such a rapid pace, how quickly you can learn (your learning agility) is actually more important than how much you know.

How quickly you can learn (your learning agility) is actually more important than how much you know.

Unfortunately, it's not hard to find examples to the contrary. In one past work assignment, I facilitated a pilot training program only to be interrupted three separate times by a newly hired manager in her forties who insisted that logging into the company intranet was too complicated and that "older employees" shouldn't be expected to learn new systems. At another event, a newly hired marketing manager was attending a development program at the company's expense and the executive leader's invitation. During the program, he stated with pride to his new peers that in the twenty years since college he hadn't read one single book.

Both of these experiences were disappointing (and embarrassing) for three reasons. First, both employees had announced publicly to their peers that they weren't interested in continuing to learn and grow. That meant their colleagues and leadership teams had every reason to doubt their current level of competence, since learning had not been a priority for them to this point. Second, both of them had placed a ceiling on their ability by refusing to grow into something more than they were at that moment. Third, both employees had just made a compelling case against ever being promoted. How can leaders develop members of their team if they won't develop themselves?

One of the best ways to stand out as a young professional is to make personal development a steady priority over the course of your career.

But what does personal growth look like as a young professional? Unlike your educational experiences growing up, there are many facets that can be included. That's what makes it so exciting! Here are several crucial areas to consider in your own growth strategy.

Experiences

For one of my final projects in graduate school, I created a corporate leadership development proposal that leveraged the wealth of knowledge possessed by Baby Boomer executives in developing their growing young professional workforce before they retired. I received an A on the assignment, but realized that if an executive team saw my presentation and tried to hire me, I'd be out of my element. I knew how to talk a good game but not how to deliver the goods.

There is simply no alternative to good old-fashioned experience. Why? Experience is the point where the rubber of theory meets the road of practice.

Experience is the point where the rubber of theory meets the road of practice.

If you want to learn something new, you need to be constantly looking to add some new experiences to your portfolio. In fact, multiple studies suggest as much as 70% of a person's professional growth comes from on-the-job experience. But keep in mind that the same experiences repeated over time don't build new competence. That's why it's important to stretch yourself, even if it's outside your comfort zone. Instead of asking how likely you are to succeed at a new experience, ask what you are likely to learn. You'll grow more that way.

Instead of asking how likely you are to succeed at a new experience, ask what you are likely to learn.

Relationships

Author and ex-Accenture colleague Robert J. Thomas observed in his book *Crucibles of Leadership* that, "no one learns alone."[17] In my estimation, there is no better way to accelerate your growth than being in close proximity with

"No one learns alone."
– Robert J. Thomas

others who are doing great work and share a commitment to learning – especially if they are a step or two ahead of you. So invest in relationships with bosses, colleagues, coaches, mentors and mentees. Pick their brains, ask questions and seek insights. Don't be obnoxious but don't let them escape without teaching you something either.

Thomas also observed that, "A great student can make a good teacher into a great teacher – and an inarticulate leader into a great teaching leader."[18] Great learners know how to get the most from the people around them.

Formal Learning

There is always a time and a place for traditional learning, whether it's a new degree, certification or corporate training program. Your organization likely has a variety of technical or professional learning programs. For most career fields, there are countless options open to the public as well.

> Don't confuse learning to know with learning to do.

In some cases, there is no substitute for formal learning. For instance, if you want to climb the ranks in accounting, at some point you'll need to complete a CPA exam. But in other situations, formal learning shouldn't be the first choice. It can be expensive and time-consuming. That's why learning goals are so important. Don't confuse learning to know with learning to do. Formal learning can teach you the first, but doesn't guarantee the second.

Feedback

The ability to receive quality feedback could be a separate book of its own. Feedback can be a difficult pill to swallow but it's worth its weight in gold. The trick is learning to accept it, ask for it and use it.[19] Ego and insecurity keep many professionals (young and seasoned) on the feedback sidelines.

Feedback can be a difficult pill to swallow, but it's worth its weight in gold.

One of the tricks I've found is to share my growth goals with someone I trust and then ask for specific feedback along the way. For example, if I'm about to give a high stakes presentation to an executive group, I might ask a colleague ahead of time to notice if my recommendations resonate with the audience members and to give me feedback afterward on how I might make them even easier to accept next time.

Not all feedback is equal, and you don't need to implement every bit you receive. But you should always consider it. And the more you ask for specific feedback, the greater quality and quantity you'll have to work with.

Assessment

Assessment doesn't get nearly the credit for growth that it should. It's a dynamic form of insight that helps measure learning progress so you can personalize and accelerate your growth goals.

For example, it's one thing to enroll in a class about customer service and receive the same training content everyone else gets. It's another thing to take a customer service assessment, identify areas of strength and opportunity for improvement and then focus on maximizing the strengths and overcoming the weaknesses. The first approach is standard. The second is personalized. The difference is incorporating assessment input into the learning process.

Some of the previously mentioned assessments, such as strengths or personality assessments, reveal natural abilities or patterns of thinking you already possess with suggested actions on how to use them more effectively. Skills-based assessments reveal proficiency gained or lacked. And learning assessments measure knowledge. And you can always use your own self-assessment against a list of competencies or your own development goals to focus your growth.

Technically speaking, assessments themselves aren't education, they're simply tools. But they generate insights that are otherwise difficult to quantify. The best way to incorporate assessments into a personal development plan is to use them to help measure and personalize your learning goals.

Environment

When I was in graduate school, I decided I wanted to work for the Chick-fil-A corporate office. Never one to pursue anything halfway, I went so far as to move to Atlanta so I could spend the summer working in a restaurant and learning the business firsthand. But before I did, I asked one of my corporate friends to recommend several franchise operators who had a well-established reputation for developing leaders who were successful with the company. I never did join Chick-fil-A's corporate team, but I did get to spend an amazing summer with operator Brad Spratte learning many lessons about business and leadership that have stuck with me to this day.

In Chapter 4, we talked about the importance of identifying the type of environments where you prefer to work, but there is a real growth consideration as well. The environments in which you spend your time will deeply shape you. They'll change you, whether you want them to or not. Have you ever seen a video of a dog that grows up with a bunch of pet rabbits? Eventually, it mimics the behavior of the environment it's in without even realizing it. The same can happen to us. The good news is we get to choose which environments we want to experience.

Individual Development Plan

Once you've developed growth goals, you need a place to record them. Many organizations will provide you with an individual development plan (IDP). Just ask your supervisor or human resources business partner where you can get one. But if they don't, you can create your own. Most IDPs have a place to include your next career goal, the particular skills you want to develop, which activities you'll commit to, timelines and support needed. A typical IDP for the year might include completing a couple classes, reading a book or handful of articles on a new work-related topic, instigating a few discussions with a mentor or performing a specific role on a new project.

If you don't have a formal IDP, you ought to create one. Create a draft and then ask your supervisor to give you feedback. Incorporate her suggestions. Regularly update it and share your progress with your supervisor as well. Try to make sure your progress gets included in your performance review discussion. This is one of the best ways you can stand out!

> It's time to commit to being a lifetime learner.

If you've treated graduation from school as the finish line for your professional growth, you're due for a new mindset. Graduation should be the starting line. It's time to commit to becoming a lifetime learner. After all, if you're not learning, you're petrifying!

Key Takeaways

1. Personal development should be a lifelong pursuit. It's a journey, not a destination.
2. How quickly you can learn (your learning agility) is more important than how much you know.
3. Experience is the most impactful growth opportunity there is, with no substitute.
4. While you can learn from anyone, the people you surround yourself with will accelerate or stunt your growth.
5. Feedback can be a difficult pill to swallow but it's worth its weight in gold.
6. Your environments will shape you – for better or worse.
7. Creating and maintaining an individual development plan (IDP) is one of the best ways to stand out as a young professional.

Discussion Questions

- What professional experiences have you learned the most from?
- What additional experiences do you need to collect in order to continue to grow?
- What are some of your personal development goals?
- What types of people do you need to spend more time with to continue to grow? Are there any specific individuals who come to mind?
- What professional feedback has been most helpful for you?
- What specific feedback can you ask for? Who can you ask?

- What type of environment do you need to find in order to accelerate your growth?
- Do you have a current IDP? What is one item that needs to be included in it?

7

Engagement – Engage Yourself with Your Organization

If you've spent any time in the corporate world, you've probably been bombarded by requests from executives and human resources to complete your annual employee engagement survey. (If your organization is progressive, you might even do this multiple times each year.) Contrary to how you may feel at times, your engagement is a high priority to the leaders in your workplace. Not only that, executives are spending more and more time, energy and financial investment trying to figure out how to engage their young professionals. After all, young professionals became the largest segment of the workforce in 2016.[20] But according to a recent Gallup study, young professionals are less engaged in the workplace than their older counterparts. In fact, 55% of Millennials are not engaged at work.[21]

Here is just a sample of the ways executives are trying to design the work experience specifically to attract, engage and retain young professionals:

- Company perks
- Workspace design
- Meeting structure
- Teaming and collaboration

- Gamifying career paths
- Work-life integration
- Executive exposure
- Succession planning

One of the big frustrations among executives is investing in new engagement initiatives only to have their top young professional talent leave for outside opportunities. Turns out "Pretzel Day" may work on *The Office*, but not every perk keeps young professionals engaged long-term. These trends will continue as expectations about what comprises an ideal work experience keep shifting.

Let's flip the script and consider engagement from your standpoint. Have you ever gotten fed up with a job and left only to find that the next one had its own issues? You might have left an unfair boss but instead you gained a nasty colleague upset you got the opportunity he was hoping for. Or you received a promotion, but it came with ten extra hours added to your weekly workload. Or your new company served up free lunch on Fridays, but you had a hard time connecting to the purpose of the organization.

Sometimes the issues we encounter are no fault of the organization, they're baggage we bring with us. In that case, new scenery won't solve the problem. After all, wherever you go, there you are.

Wherever you go, there you are.

While we're on the topic, let me point out that if you didn't participate in your last employee engagement survey and provide suggestions, you're helping to maintain the status quo.

At some point, we need to honestly consider the question: whose responsibility is *your* engagement?

> It's your responsibility to engage yourself with your organization.

Your organization has a vested interest in engaging you at work. They invest time, energy and resources each year to this effect. They don't always get it right, but it's a constant priority. But engagement is a two-way street. It's your responsibility to engage yourself with your organization.

What does engaging yourself look like in action? Here are some ways you can begin.

Know Your Engagement Factors

When I joined Accenture's management consulting practice, one of the activities they requested every year was for each of us to consider a list of engagement factors, rank them in order of our preferences and then rate them according to our level of engagement. Then they collected the information in order to adapt their engagement initiatives to match our preferences. But the real value was the clarity the exercise created for us.

Take a look at the engagement factors below. How would you rank and rate them?

- People you work with and for
- Interesting and meaningful work
- Growth opportunities
- Work environment
- Company brand
- Rewards and recognition

Are you engaged in your job? It's a lot more nuanced of a question when you evaluate it through the lens of multiple factors. Maybe you don't love your boss, but you also can't get enough of the fascinating work. Maybe the company brand isn't strong, but you have more growth opportunities than you can count.

As I've mentioned already, it's easy to react to what we don't like but difficult to know what we really want. That's why it's so important to know what engages us most.

What Makes a Good Day at Work?

How often do you leave for the day down about something at work? What about the days you leave motivated and excited? Do you take the time to reflect and document why you feel the way you do?

In his book *The 15 Invaluable Laws of Growth*, John Maxwell writes that experience is a hard teacher because the test is given first and the lesson is given afterward. But unless you are intentional about evaluating the experience, there's a good chance of missing out on the lesson![22]

In other words, it's not experience alone but *evaluated* experience that is the best teacher.

> It's not experience alone but *evaluated* experience that is the best teacher.

The simplest way to evaluate your experience at work is to take three minutes at the end of each day and rate your day on a 1 to 10 scale. Then write a short rationale for the score. I'm not talking a full journal, just a running list on your note taking app with a bullet point or two. At the end of each month, look through your list and see if any trends stand out to you. Are there any recurring themes? If you scored higher or lower than usual, what might have changed?

What Can You Do to Engage Yourself?

I've never met a young professional who enjoyed leaving money on the table after a salary negotiation. But I'm convinced that's what frequently occurs when it comes to engagement. We rarely take everything our organization has to offer us.

At a new leader orientation session I facilitated recently, one new manager shared a story of a past supervisor who inspired her. He saw her potential when she was a student and insisted that she come work for him after she graduated. She went on to recount how he provided her with a special opportunity to step up and prove herself, and it ended up leading to her new leadership role.

"Actually," she corrected herself, mid-story, "The opportunity was available to all of us. I guess I was the only one who took it."

Another time, a young Army specialist complained to me that his superiors weren't paying attention to his special skills or assigning him work that matched his credentials. "Have you raised your hand and told them about your qualifications?" I asked. "Have you asked to be assigned any of the jobs you're interested in?" He hadn't up to that point.

As both of these young professionals illustrated, having an opportunity is one thing, but taking it is another. We all have the opportunity to act on our own insights with regard to engagement. Once you're armed with real-time information about which factors engage you the most and what a good day at work looks like, it begs the question: who has the most control over whether you're engaged at work – you or your organization?

If you like what you're getting, keep doing what you're doing.

If you don't, take action. What can you do to get more of what you want and less of what you don't?

If you like some areas but think others could be improved, that's your opportunity to take ownership and self-direct your experience.

It's true that the current generation of young professionals is known as the "gig generation," shuffling between jobs at breakneck speed in the hopes of finding greener grass. Sometimes it results in better opportunities. But when it doesn't, there's a good chance there was a missed opportunity.

Your current organization may contain hidden treasure as it relates to engagement. Don't give up too soon! Do the thoughtful, proactive work to take ownership of your own engagement. Your organization is already working on their part. Are you doing yours? You have everything to gain if you do.

> Your current organization may contain hidden treasure as it relates to engagement. Don't give up too soon!

Key Takeaways

1. It's your responsibility to engage yourself with your organization.
2. To be engaged, know what factors engage you most.
3. Evaluate the quality of your daily experiences and choose positive experiences to add to your day.
4. Be proactive instead of waiting for your organization to improve things for you.
5. Complete your organization's employee engagement survey – it's the very least you can do to influence positive change.

Discussion Questions

- What is your organization currently doing to engage you in your work experience?
- Did you complete your last employee engagement survey? If so, what suggestions did you provide?
- What organization-provided perk do you appreciate most that you couldn't get just anywhere?
- Of the engagement factors listed above, which is the most important for you? Least?
- When you have a good day at work, what is the most frequent reason? What about a bad day?
- What is one way you can better engage yourself with your organization?

8

Team Focus – We Before Me

When I joined the military as part of the Army special operations community, one of the first things my fellow soldiers and I learned was the four "SOF Truths." (SOF is short for "Special Operations Forces.") One SOF Truth is, "humans are more important than hardware." Another is, "Special Operations Forces cannot be mass produced."[23]

It wasn't until a couple years later that I learned there was actually a fifth SOF Truth that hadn't been shared in my initial training: "Most special operations require non-SOF assistance."

That meant SOF couldn't be successful on most missions without their non-SOF counterparts – even though non-SOF personnel didn't have to go through the same level of training or operate in the same "special" community.

A few years later, as a consultant to the FBI, I quickly noticed an underlying "us" vs. "them" cultural tension between the special agent workforce and the professional staff. There must be something about the word "special" that makes teamwork more difficult!

For young professionals, this poses a particularly significant paradox. Based on generational trends regarding our upbringing, most young professionals today have been conditioned to pursue a form of self-actualization. The underlying message "you can be anything you want to be" that Millennials and Generation Z grew up hearing is positive, affirming and empowering – all good things. The challenge comes when a group of confident, self-determined individuals join an organization and begin to work together. The success of the organization depends on the performance of its teams. The question quickly becomes: what will it take for these individuals to work together as one?

Teamwork is the next great competitive advantage.

I'm convinced that teamwork is the next great competitive advantage. The young professionals who achieve greatness will be the ones who learn how to be great teammates, even if it means playing a support role from time to time. After all, the new leadership paradigm depends on everyone – regardless of title or position – accepting the responsibility to lead, influence, support and follow when the situation calls for it.

The Language of Teamwork

Duke University men's basketball coach Mike Krzyzewski ("Coach K") could teach a clinic on teamwork, even without a basketball or a clipboard. In his book *Leading with the Heart*, Coach K uses the perfect analogy to distinguish between the potential of a team and an individual: a hand. Outstretched, each finger is vulnerable and alone, but clenched, they're firm and powerful. The strongest, most talented finger is no match for a fist. When it comes to teamwork, it's not individual talent that matters. It's the unity, commitment and combined performance of the team.

According to Coach K, one of the best ways to adapt to a team identity is to adopt inclusive language. That means it's important to use plural pronouns right away.[24]

From "I" to "we"
From "my" to "our"
From "me" to "us."

For team players, it's never "my" team. It's always "our" team. As Coach K says, only a group mentality can create a team identity. The bottom line is this: win or lose, teams work together. When they don't, the team competes with itself instead of with the opponent.

> "Only a group mentality can create a team identity."
> – Coach K

Chief Collaborators

As a young professional, it may seem as though the executive ranks will forever be out of reach. But there is one executive role that is available immediately: Chief Collaboration Officer.

One of my past colleagues, Adam, demonstrated his affinity for this role with a self-initiated side project. He noticed a group of regionally dispersed business partners who seemed disconnected from the corporate function and each other. Even though he wasn't in charge, Adam took the initiative to schedule regular collaboration calls. The meetings quickly evolved into think tanks and best practice sharing. Since he worked in the corporate office, when someone had questions, Adam went the extra mile to track down the person with the answer and follow up with the group.

> Chief collaborators anticipate the information others need that they have access to and go out of their way to provide it.

Chief collaborators anticipate the information

others need that they have access to and go out of their way to provide it.

You don't need special skills or authority to be a chief collaboration officer. The role is open to anyone. You may not be offered a corner office for your efforts, but using your collaboration imagination is exactly the type of behavior team players exhibit. It's one of the best ways to stand out!

Be Good at Making Others Look Good

I'll never forget a conversation I had with Janet Kamerman. At the time she was the Chief Learning Officer of the FBI and about to be promoted even higher up the career ladder. I was a junior member of a consulting team working on a short-term project. What started as a quick banter in the hallway after a meeting turned into a deep philosophical epiphany for me when Janet described the type of leader the Bureau needed to be more effective.

"We need leaders who are good," Janet stated... "at making *other people* look good."

What a dichotomy. Most of us focus on being good and looking good ourselves and stop there. We need to be good at making *other people* look good.

Be good at making other people look good.

Author and chief executive Cheryl Bachelder took that idea a step further. In her bestselling book *Dare to Serve*, Bachelder shares the analogy of the spotlight.[25] Confident and secure leaders are content to share and even focus the spotlight onto others. They thrive off shared, not seized, opportunities.

Pardon the basketball analogy, but when was the last time you passed up a slam dunk to toss an alley-oop to one of your teammates? That's what team players who are worth following do.

It's rare to find a team that remains intact for long. New opportunities come and take star performers away to tackle new challenges. The only way to stay effective is to get comfortable using your teaming skills. After all, poor teamwork means beating yourself instead of the competition.

We can accomplish even more when we work for each other.

At the end of the day, self-actualization is a worthy aim but can also be a lonely path. Why is it that we're more inspired by a video clip of an athlete who stops to help an injured competitor than one who finishes in first place? The good news is we can accomplish even more when we work for each other.

How do I know this?

"A confidence shared is better than a confidence only in yourself."
– Coach K

Perhaps Coach K put it best when he said, "A confidence shared is better than a confidence only in yourself."[26]

I used to be afraid of feeling little
I used to never wanna play a second fiddle
But that all changed when I met you

I don't need the spotlight
I just wanna see you shine

— Ben Rector, Duo

Key Takeaways

1. Teamwork is the next great competitive advantage.
2. Teamwork beats individual talent every single time.
3. Great teams use inclusive language.
4. Be proactive about providing information and resources to the people around you.
5. Be good at making other people look good. Share the spotlight instead of seizing it for yourself.

Discussion Questions

- What was the best team you were ever part of? What made it great?
- What was the worst team you were ever part of? What was the problem?
- What is your personal teamwork "quotient?" To an organization that values teamwork, how attractive of a teammate are you?
- Evaluate your language – what's one team-inclusive phrase or statement you need to start using?
- What information do you have that someone else would benefit from? How can you provide it?
- Who can you make look good? How will you do this?

9

Career Savvy – Be the Employee Every Organization Wants

Growing up, the underlying purpose of education seemed to be preparation to join the workforce and become responsible, contributing members of society. Maybe it was never stated in those words exactly, but I knew from early on my parents didn't want me living with them forever! What was missing was any conversation either at home or in school about what to do *after* getting a job. What was supposed to come next? Or were things just supposed to work themselves out from there?

For me, my first job was just the starting point. Finding a job I loved came next. Then figuring out how to specialize – and then, how to advance. But the questions kept coming. What does it take to manage a career well?

It wasn't long into my job with Accenture that I was given what might have been the most impactful career advice I've ever received: "Your career is your responsibility."

Your career is your responsibility.

No pressure, right?

The good news is that we can all be the young professionals our organizations and industries desire, provided we're willing to step up and accept the challenge.

Be Known Positively

Did you know there is a conversation about you that is currently taking place among your superiors in your organization? Turns out, you're not anonymous. You can't control much of what is said, but you can influence it. Your personal brand counts double at the leadership level. It requires being able to step outside of your own shoes and view yourself from the standpoint of those leaders. What is most important to them? What do they want most from you?

In my book *Ignite Your Leadership Expertise*, I write about the importance of making life easier, less complicated and more fun for those you serve.[27] It sounds simplistic and a little cheesy, but to the degree you can pull it off, you'll be seen (and discussed) in a positive light.

Go Above and Beyond

What does high performance look like in your role? It's very difficult to do more than expected unless you know what the expectations are to begin with.

Here's a quick tip: when you set your performance goals for the year, ask your boss which ones are worth the most bonus money at the end of the year. She may be surprised at first, but will usually quickly point to one or two of them. Make those your top priority – and work hard to exceed them.

Here's an even bigger tip: constantly ask to take work off your boss's plate. Not all bosses do a great job letting their teams know what projects they are working on. But always assume they are even busier than you are.

Make Something Better for Everyone

I'll let you in on a little secret I've learned. It takes a lot of work to change the world. It's a lot of work to change anything, really. But at any given time, there are dozens of projects the leaders in your organization wish they could get to. They simply don't have the time and attention. That's your big area of opportunity. If you can find a way to make something better for everyone – even if it's just a little thing – don't be surprised if some big kudos come your way. This is a great visibility and teamwork opportunity as well.

Build Competence at the Next Level

One of the biggest career mistakes young professionals make is assuming they're ready for a promotion too soon. They've mastered their current role so they must be ready for the next one, right? Wrong. Being good at your job means just that – you're good where you are. You must demonstrate ability at the next level in order to win the opportunity.

Don't wait until you think you're ready for the next role to start preparing for it. Ask for a competency list or job description for one (or several) roles of interest at the next level. Determine which experiences, skills, development or relationships you need to be ready and incorporate them into your individual development plan. Involve your boss early and ask for regular input as you go. Your conversations will go even better if you're exceeding your goals in your current role – that's why delivering results are so important.

Subtle Self-Promotion

No one likes a showoff, but visibility is a prerequisite for bigger and better opportunities. If your leadership team doesn't know about the work you're contributing, they can't judge in your favor. It's tricky since younger generations already have a reputation for entitlement. But visibility is a necessity as well. So how can you pull it off with grace and poise?

Another tip I share in my book *Ignite Your Leadership Expertise* is how to appropriately toot your own horn. It's this: subtly self-promote areas of competence and achievement.[28] Be humble and hungry, patient and proactive. What this looks like practically is letting teammates and superiors know what they should depend on you for, highlighting your past work and offering to help in similar ways. It's thinking ahead and coming to meetings with recommendations already prepared. It's keeping track of your accomplishments and asking your boss for opportunities to get an even bigger win next time.

Be humble and hungry, patient and proactive.

Ask for Help

At a team meeting a few years ago, we diagnosed what was working well, what wasn't and what we should change. Our biggest takeaway was that everyone wanted greater individual support, but no one wanted to ask for it.

I've never met anyone who wanted to appear incompetent, but it's a sign of insecurity not to ask for help when you need it. And at the risk of pointing out the obvious, if you don't ask for what you need, it's a lot harder to get it. When you do, you just might find that others need the same support as you and will appreciate your courage.

If you don't ask for what you need, it's a lot harder to get it.

Be as resourceful as you can be. Solve issues at the lowest level possible. But ask for help when you need it so you can make a stronger contribution.

Ask for What You Want

In a similar fashion, it's important to ask for what you want, even if it feels intimidating at first. Initiating high stakes *in-person* conversations isn't usually a strong point for most young professionals, at least not initially. The squeaky wheel tends to get the grease, but the trick is to squeak appropriately.

There will be times when you need to share your desire for a new project, a different role, an expensive development opportunity, a raise, a promotion or any number of other changes. The best way to start a career discussion with your boss is to make it a periodic two-way conversation rather than an unexpected confrontation. Offer your fact-based self-assessment, ask for what you want and then ask for your boss's assessment of your assessment. If you're way off, ask how you can set more realistic expectations for yourself. Either way, ask to continue the conversation at an appropriate (and specific) time.

You owe it to both yourself and your organization to give them an opportunity to give you what you want, especially if the alternative is to jump ship to another employer. You won't always get it, but you should always take the chance. Given the choice to speak up too soon or too late, err on the side of too soon. Whatever you do, don't let fear or intimidation get in your way. Don't worry about saying everything quite right – you probably won't. It's all part of the learning process and you'll get a little better each time.

You owe it to both yourself and your organization to give them an opportunity to give you what you want, especially if the alternative is to jump ship to another employer.

Bounce Back

I'm not going to sugarcoat it, the world of work is a tough place. You'll be disappointed and possibly disillusioned more than once. Sometimes it'll be your fault. Sometimes it won't.

I love what former NFL coach John Fox said about these types of moments. "Sometimes setbacks are setups for greater things to come."

"Sometimes setbacks are setups for greater things to come."
– John Fox

If you expect to encounter a few setbacks here and there, and determine in advance to learn from them, grow and keep moving, they won't have the power to keep you down long. Don't turn into the seasoned professional who still won't let go of his early career bumps and bruises.

WWAMYPD?

There's one question I'm convinced can solve 99% of all young professional challenges. It's not a question about best practice or what you want most. It's not even about what's right or wrong. It's simply this:

What would a mature young professional do?

What would a mature young professional do?

The answer is usually obvious but requires us to step up our character, sometimes more than we've been willing to do up till now. Take the next step – it'll always be worth it. After all, maturity never has an age limit. You're never too young to set a good example. Be the mature young professional in the room, and you'll always stand out!

That's enough to keep any young professional busy for quite a while. But if you'd like more, check out my bonus resource *20 Ways to Be More (Young) Professional* at the end of the book or at www.nathanmagnuson.com/resources. (Hint: It makes a great 20-day challenge as well!)

Key Takeaways

1. Your career is your responsibility.
2. Your superiors are already talking about you and it's up to you to give them positive things to say.
3. It's impossible to excel in your career without quality performance.
4. You must demonstrate proficiency at the next level before you can expect to earn a promotion.
5. Know what you want your organization to do for you and be confident enough to ask for it.
6. Expect periodic setbacks and they will be easier to handle and overcome.
7. Ask what a mature young professional would do in your situation and you'll solve 99% of your problems.

Discussion Questions

- What can you do to be known more positively in your organization?
- What work can you take off your boss's plate starting right now?
- What is one core area of competence? How can you subtly self-promote it, and to whom?
- Where do you need to ask for help right now?
- What do you want your next career step to be? Is it a step up or a lateral move? Is it inside your organization or outside?
- Have you ever botched a career discussion? What would you have done differently?
- How would a mature young professional approach a particular challenge you're dealing with?

10

Leadership – What to Do When You (Finally) Get Put in Charge

In the years since I began studying what makes leaders effective, I've come to realize there are two instances when most of us begin thinking about leadership. The first is when we experience poor leadership for the first time. We might encounter a coach who reacts negatively in little league sports or a teacher who makes a poor decision in elementary school. Without thinking, we assume we're an expert on what good leadership looks like.

The second instance is when we experience our first leadership challenge. All of a sudden, leadership doesn't seem quite so simple after all!

As a young professional, you may be wondering if your opportunity to lead from the front will ever arrive. All I can say is: get ready. Demographic and economic factors indicate your chance will come sooner rather than later, likely well before you're fully prepared. Baby Boomers will continue to retire in droves and low unemployment rates, while great for job seekers, create a leadership vacuum for organizations, including at the executive leadership ranks. Simply put: leadership demand far outweighs leadership supply. But isn't that always the case?

> "If you stay ready, you don't need to get ready."
>
> – Will Smith

If you're waiting until you get promoted to figure out how to lead, you're already sorely behind. Getting thrown off the deep end of a new leadership assignment can be a nightmare if you haven't yet learned to swim. That's why leadership preparation is crucial for success, even before your opportunity arrives. As actor Will Smith noted, "If you stay ready, you don't need to get ready."

When you take ownership and develop a winning mindset, that's personal leadership. When you put "we" before "me," that's team leadership. But leading from a position of authority is its own frontier. Let me share a preview of what's most important in your first leadership role (or any new leadership role) so you can begin the preparation now.

Understand the Situation

Late author and executive Max De Pree eloquently stated in his masterful book *Leadership is an Art*, "The first responsibility of a leader is to define reality. The last is to say thank you."[29]

We'll talk about appreciation in a bit, but let's start with defining reality.

When you're in a new leadership role, it's critical to understand the situation you are walking in to. Is the team well-resourced and focused on maintaining the status quo? Is the organization in rapid growth mode with everyone just trying to keep up? Is it in the midst of a transformation? Who are the biggest stakeholders and what is their level of engagement?

Hopefully you've gained a clear understanding of the situation during the transition stage, but nothing can prepare you 100% until you begin. The longer you go without clear goals, the harder it gets to create your own clarity. When you understand the situation, you can adapt your approach to meet the real needs, instead of the other way around.

Incidentally, the best way to understand any situation (whether you're a new leader or not) is by asking great questions![30]

Win Early and Often

When you finally get the chance to lead from the front, a quick win goes a long way. Visibility shouldn't be the main goal, but achieving a positive and visible outcome quickly significantly enhances 360 degree confidence. Quick wins snowball into greater credibility and sustained results.

> Quick wins snowball into new credibility and sustained results.

Recounting her past leadership shortcomings as president of KFC, author and chief executive Cheryl Bachelder admitted that she had failed to fully appreciate senior leadership's urgency for getting quick results, focusing instead on creating a long-term strategy. The misplaced focus ultimately backfired, and she was replaced.[31] Fortunately, Bachelder used the painful experience to lead a turnaround as CEO of Popeyes Louisiana Kitchen where she initiated bold, visible, quick and prioritized improvements. The result? Popeyes increased their adjusted stock price from $17 per share when she took over to $79 per share when she departed ten years later.[32]

> The right time to get positive results is early and often.

The right time to get positive results is early and often.

Make the Tough Calls

Being the one to make important decisions looks fun from the outside. We picture ourselves behind a large desk with a line of people waiting for our astute judgment – or something like that. It's anything but. Substitute the word "important" with "difficult" and you'll have a more realistic picture. Tough decisions, by definition, are tough. There's usually more grey area lined with uncertainty than black and white. Rarely will everyone be happy with the outcome. And many times, it's just not that much fun!

In one new job where I'd accepted a leadership role, I found out a young colleague had recently returned to work from a serious injury. Her previous job had been filled when she was out on medical leave and she'd been placed temporarily on my team. Now that I was there, I needed to make the difficult decision of how to handle her employment status. We hadn't budgeted for an additional person, so it soon became evident it was my responsibility as the leader to facilitate her exit from the organization. Fortunately, we were able to hire her back into a different role after the fact, but it didn't make the decision-making process any less painful on my end.

Unfortunately, not all leaders possess the courage to make difficult decisions. They'd rather play it safe and push the risk and responsibility up the chain of command. Eventually the leaders at the top wonder why they have to make all the decisions around here. What's the point of having leaders if nobody will act like one?

Accepting the responsibility to make the tough calls means you'll be unpopular, disliked and *wrong* from time to time. It won't take long before you'll earn the scars to prove it. Not only that, the reward for making tough decisions is even tougher decisions in the future. Ready or not... it's time to lead.

The reward for making tough decisions is even tougher decisions in the future.

By the way, because decision-making is such a critical skillset for young professionals, I dedicated one of my bonuses to the topic. It's called *Decision-Making Hacks for Young Professionals* and you can learn more at the back of the book or at www.nathanmagnuson.com/resources.

Develop Your Team

If the best teammates are good at making other people look good, then the most effective bosses set their focus beyond individual leadership performance to developing the leadership potential of others. At the end of the day, leaders are only as successful as the collective skills, performance and collaboration of their teams.

Developing talent means growing the competence and confidence of the people around you. Sometimes you'll be the expert who sets the course but delegates the execution. Other times they'll be the expert and you'll need to trust their capability. You'll need to direct, coach, support and encourage. You'll need to initiate constructive feedback. You'll need to exercise extreme patience at times. It will require extra time, energy and discipline. Many leaders can't bring themselves to let go of the details and address every issue themselves, effectively placing a lid on their own leadership capacity. Others won't step out of their comfort zones or give up their pet projects. Equipping and empowering others to execute is the only way to reach new heights, even when they make mistakes that you have to take accountability for. You'll graduate to higher levels of leadership only when you're capable of developing a talented team.

When you're the leader, your own individual talent, when over-relied on over time, can become your kryptonite.

When you're the leader, your own individual talent, when over-relied on over time, can become your kryptonite.

Stand and Applaud

One of my all-time favorite quotes comes from 18th century English poet Samuel Johnson, who said, "The applause of a single human being is of great consequence." Modern day employee engagement research backs Johnson's claim, especially when coming from a supervisor. According to Gallup, only 30% of employees strongly agree that they've recently received recognition or praise for doing good work.[33]

"The applause of a single human being is of great consequence."

– Samuel Johnson

In my book *Ignite Your Leadership Expertise*, I share that when you win someone's heart, they will give you their mind as well.[34] You won't know true leadership success until you've helped your followers test their wings and then stood back and applauded their flight.

If you have to ask yourself if you've given enough praise and recognition lately, you haven't. Start today, and once you do, never quit. If there's one thing to be obnoxious about, it's showing genuine appreciation.

> If there's one thing to be obnoxious about, it's showing genuine appreciation.

Leadership isn't for the faint of heart. It'll test the very core of your being more than once. Leadership is a higher calling. Lead well, and you'll make one of the largest contributions a person can make simply because being well led is one of the greatest gifts a person can receive.

Remember, as a young professional, your time to lead will come – probably sooner than you think.

Perhaps Robert J. Thomas said it best, "Sometimes events can conspire to make you a leader."[35]

When your time comes to lead, will you accept the challenge?

Key Takeaways

1. You will likely be called upon to lead before you are ready, not after.
2. Not all leadership situations are the same and it's crucial that you recognize which one you're being asked to lead.
3. There is no such thing as certainty when making difficult decisions, but the leader's job is to make them anyway.
4. When leaders fail to develop their teams, they place a lid on their own leadership.
5. If there's one thing to be obnoxious about, it's showing genuine appreciation.
6. Leading well is one of the greatest contributions a person can make.

Discussion Questions

- Which leadership challenge applies to you: getting antsy while you play the waiting game, reluctant to accept the next challenge or struggling to navigate the new leadership opportunity you've been given?
- What's the most impactful leadership lesson you've learned so far on your journey?
- How well do you understand the leadership situation you're in?
- What is the toughest leadership decision you've had to make so far?
- Is giving praise and recognition easy or difficult for you?
- Who is one person who deserves your appreciation? When will you give it?

Conclusion

As college students, my classmate Keelan and I would take breaks from comparing study notes to discuss all the businesses we wanted to start someday. The possibilities were endless and we couldn't wait to carve out a place for ourselves in the professional world. Unfortunately, we both spent our first few years after graduation working in low-paying jobs that didn't fit our strengths or interests. The desire and work ethic were present, but it was pretty frustrating having to figure out how to find our way by ourselves.

Fast forward a decade. Keelan and I still talk about all the businesses we hope to start someday. But we also talk about the winding path, risks and tough decisions that landed us in much better places. We're working within our desired fields, doing work we care about (and are good at) and earning higher salaries than we expected when we first got started. If you would have told us in college the things we'd be doing today, I doubt either of us would have believed you. "I wish I would've known back then what I know now – especially that these things were available to me," we've remarked on more than one occasion.

I'd like to think we're just getting warmed up for what's yet to come.

Maybe you were fortunate enough to have been given a realistic idea about what is available for you right from the start. Or like my friend Keelan and I, your path hit several speed bumps and detours along the way. Hopefully this message comes at the right time for you. Keep going. The process is worth it. The possibilities truly are endless.

If you've made it this far, you've realized this book is much more than a set of tips and tricks to get to the next step. It's truly about your own "path to becoming." All that you are and can become is still in the process of being pursued, discovered and realized.

None of us will be young professionals forever. That's why the time in our twenties and thirties is such a gift. When it's all said and done and we reach the sunset stage of life, all the jobs (dream jobs and otherwise), adventures, projects, aspirations and deadlines will start to fade. What will matter most at that point is who we became, what we contributed, who we served, how well we loved and what legacy we left behind.

What will your legacy from your young professional years be? What will you learn and contribute? Whose lives will you impact? Who will you become in the process? You're the only one who can make that determination.

Go forth with anticipation.
Take the next step with boldness.
Run with perseverance.
Win with honor.
Reflect with honesty.
Lead with courage.

Okay... now that you've made it to the end, congratulations! But the fun isn't over yet. Here are a few next steps you can take to maximize the value of this adventure.

- **Step 1 – Check out the bonus materials.** The *20 Ways to Be More (Young) Professional* bonus is included in the next section and you can download it as well at www.nathanmagnuson.com/resources. It makes a great 20-day challenge! You can also download the other two bonus resources: *Decision-Making Hacks for Young Professionals* and *How to Win the Hearts of Your Young Professionals*.

- **Step 2 – Lead a book club at work.** Now that you've read the book, you're in the perfect position to start a book club with your young professional colleagues. The ten chapters fit neatly into a 10 week book club. If funding is a barrier, ask your supervisor, HR leader or an executive with a soft spot for young professionals if they will sponsor the group. You might even invite them to stop by and offer their own words of wisdom.
- **Step 3 – Share this book with leadership.** Your organization has a vested interest in attracting, engaging, developing and retaining young professionals like you. But they don't always know where to find the best resources. Show your supervisor, HR leader, training leader or department executive the Table of Contents for this book and share what you learned. Another great resource to share with this group is the *5 Ways to Win the Hearts of Your Young Professionals* bonus resource which is designed to help them engage you. It'll be a win-win!
- **Step 4 – Visit the website.** Visit www.nathanmagnuson.com to view my latest young professional updates. You can even subscribe to receive my newly published articles.
- **Step 5 – Request a speaking or training experience.** If you liked the book but want to go

deeper, ask your organization's leadership to invest in their young professionals by requesting a speaking or training experience. Our young professional training sessions are highly interactive and bring to life many of the topics included in this book. You can learn more about our corporate training by visiting my website or by contacting me via email at nathan@nathanmagnuson.com.

- **Step 6 – Share on social media.** Keep the conversation going! You can certainly follow my social media posts or share any of the numerous quotes and quips included in this book. But follow and share other sources and your own insights as well. And makes sure to include the hashtag #youngprofessionals. The more we can continue to positively raise awareness for young professional issues in the workplace (especially ways we want to enhance our contributions), the more support we'll receive.

BONUS #1

20 Ways to Be More (Young) Professional

Have you ever heard young professionals criticized for their lack of professionalism? Maybe you've been on the receiving end of a professionalism lecture a time or two. Why is professionalism so important? Easy. It's hard to stand out (in a positive way) if your professionalism is in question.

Professionalism means many different things to different people. We usually think of dressing appropriately and behaving in group settings. That's probably a good place to start. But there's more to it than that, especially for young professionals.

In my book *Stand Out! Become a Young Professional Who Wins at Work and Life*, I mention that you're never too young to set a good example. These twenty professionalism tips are excerpted from the book. Master them and no one will have reason to doubt your credibility. In fact, you'll stand out – for all the right reasons!

On the other hand, if you're a leader of young professionals, these twenty tips may be just what you need to encourage your team.

1. Focus on What You *Can* Do

The more green you are, the less you're capable of delivering. But that shouldn't stop you from providing great service to those you work with. Instead of focusing on what you *can't* do (due to lack of skill or team capacity), redirect the focus to what you *can* do. In other words, be known for saying, "yes" to what you can confidently and competently deliver, even if it takes some creativity to get there.

2. Be an Early Bird, Late Owl

One of the greatest laments about young professionals in the workplace is their lack of reliability for when they show up for work. This means if all you do is arrive and leave on time, you'll stand out from the pack in a positive way! Take it a step further by arriving early and leaving late. You don't need to put in extra hours. Even giving five minutes on either end – with the ability to flex extra when needed – further enhances your reliability.

3. Dress to Impress

In many consulting companies, the dress code is to meet or exceed the standards of the clients they serve. The reason is simple: it's hard to take people seriously when they are underdressed. You can certainly maintain your own sense of style, but don't hurt your credibility by looking like a ragamuffin. If in doubt, it always pays to ask a colleague or supervisor for their opinion. They will appreciate your inquiry. If you ever receive negative feedback on the professionalism of your outfit, make it a goal to never let it happen again.

4. Get Mini-Mentors

Anyone who knows more than you about a certain subject has the potential to serve as a mentor. All you need to do is ask. But instead of asking for an ambiguous, long-term commitment to your success, ask for 30 minutes to pose a few specific questions. Then find another mini-mentor on another subject. If you don't ask, the answer is always no. And always, *always* say thank you!

5. Grow and Support Your Network

There's a saying about networking that "it's not who you know, but who who you know knows" that has the ability to open the right door. It's hard to understate the value of a quality network. Always take the initiative to build and collect new relationships. You don't need to establish deep connections with each new person you meet, and you don't need to have a specific request when you do. In fact, it's more important to offer to be a resource for them and add value to their efforts. Take pride in connecting the people you meet with others who can solve their problems or meet their needs.

6. Use, "Yes, And"

"No" is no fun. Yes is not always possible. And nothing good comes after using, "but." When you disagree or see things differently, resist the urge to say, "no." Even better, resist saying, "yes, *but*...." Instead, use, "yes... *and*..." to allow both yourself and the others the opportunity to consider a different perspective.

7. Drop the Gossip

You don't need to become a robotic "yes man" for the team or organization you work with. Contributing your own point-of-view and attempting to analyze decisions made by others is one of the best ways to challenge your own perspective and deepen your understanding. But starting or passing along information that paints others in a negative light can cause irreversible damage, especially if you're only working from hearsay or your own assumptions. One of the quickest ways to make enemies is to speak poorly of others when they aren't around. If in doubt, keep your thoughts about other people to yourself. Better yet, commit to never speaking ill of others in the first place!

8. Be a People Person

Jack Welch said, "If you don't like people, leadership stinks!"[36] I think that includes many aspects of being a professional as well. One unfortunate trend among young professionals today is a preference for interacting via technology instead of face-to-face. It's up to you to learn to make a human connection – even if you need to force yourself at times. The American marketplace rewards extroversion. Even if you are shy, make the decision to become genuinely interested in others. Then act on that initiative. Say hello to someone new and find out what is important to them. Go to someone's desk to interact in-person once in a while. Pick up the phone instead of hiding behind email when you need information. When people know who you are, they are more likely to appreciate you and want to work together.

9. Smile

How much is a smile worth? Charles Schwab estimated that his was worth $1 million. Yours is worth a lot too. That's because of everything a smile communicates. A smile says many things, including, "I'm a positive person," "I'm happy with who I am," "I care about you more than my own problems," "I have your best interest in mind," and "Let's work together."[37]

10. Ask for Feedback

Feedback is a wonderful tool, no matter your level of experience and there are many ways to maximize the quality of the feedback you receive. But for young professionals, feedback provides a key additional benefit – it demonstrates humility and a willingness to learn from others. Don't be shy about asking for feedback, even (and especially) from those further along than you. Just make sure it is specific. Simply asking, "Do you mind if I get your input about something?" is a great way to begin.

11. Learn to Ask Great Questions

Many young professionals are intimidated about looking foolish and are anxious to prove they know at least some of the answers. Those opportunities will come with experience. But in the meantime, gain a reputation for asking great questions. In my book *Ignite Your Leadership Expertise*, I share how great questions develop strong listening and critical thinking skills and lead to great discoveries. Questions help put process between opportunity and decision. You don't need to know all the answers to make a meaningful contribution. So collect and ask great questions.

12. Follow Up When You Don't Know

"I don't know the answer right now, but I'll find it and get back with you." As a young professional, there will be plenty of times when you won't know the answer. There's no shame in that. In fact, in the knowledge age, being able to find an answer is actually more valuable than knowing the answer.

But not knowing doesn't let you off the hook from providing a high quality service experience. Provide follow-up promptly and accurately.

13. Develop Business Acumen

Are you a generalist or a specialist? There's no one right answer – the workforce needs both. But whatever you are, it's important to gain exposure to other areas of the organization, and especially the business fundamentals. Everyone ought to learn the basics of financial management, customer service, employee engagement, data analytics and the core services your organization provides. Go out of your way to build your business acumen – otherwise you may need to wait longer than you want for a promotion opportunity.

14. Focus on the Result

Peter Drucker famously observed, "Efficiency is doing things right; effectiveness is doing the right things." Activity doesn't equal accomplishment. There are many ways you could be spending your time at work. The less experience you have, the more you must rely on the direction someone else sets for you. But as you develop your expertise, pay special attention to the intended outcome of your work. If you're not sure your activity is achieving the desired result, don't be afraid to raise your hand and ask.

15. Put the Customer First

Do you serve your organization's customers directly? Or do you work in a support role? Who are your team's biggest stakeholders? Just as it's important to focus on the result, it's important to filter your efforts through the lens of what is most important to the customer. For every task you complete, you should be able to articulate why it matters to the customer. If not, it's your responsibility to ask.

16. Take Work Off Your Boss's Plate

One of your main goals in any job should be to make your boss successful. Not all bosses are great at communicating how they spend their time to their staff. But it's safe to assume they have more plates to spin than you do. One of the best ways to stand out is to stand up – and offer to take on more work. If you're good at identifying efficiency opportunities, you'll be able to make the time.

17. Provide a Recommendation

Many a frustrated supervisor has implored their staff, "Don't come to me with a problem unless you also bring a solution." There's actually an even better approach you can take. Put on your consultant's hat and come with a few options to solve the problem as well as a recommendation. There's no better way to develop your critical thinking skills and demonstrate initiative. Even if your supervisor doesn't take your recommendation, he or she will appreciate your initiative – and you'll always learn more in the process.

18. Grow Your Empathy

Did you know you can demonstrate empathy even if you don't have a naturally empathetic personality? It's one of the most important skills you can develop. At its most basic level, empathy is the ability to relate to the feelings and experiences of others. One of the best ways to demonstrate empathy is to thank your customers and coworkers for sharing both their positive and negative experiences and acknowledge briefly *how that must have felt* before providing a response.

19. Let Things Go

If anyone told you work would be all fun and games, you were sorely misled. You'll collect some painful experiences as you go, simply because people are human. We all make mistakes and let each other down from time to time. There are many ways to respond. One is to have a meltdown in the moment. Another is to hold a grudge over time. A positive response to occasional painful experiences is to expect them, accept them and continue on. The quicker you can let go, the quicker you can return your focus to your next meaningful endeavor.

20. Say "Thank You"

Elton John sang, "Sorry seems to be the hardest word." But the workplace reality is that the words "thank you" appear to be just as difficult. Employees of all generations remain unengaged, feel undervalued and leave for outside opportunities simply because they feel unappreciated. Saying "thank you" ought to become second nature to the point that it flies off your tongue. Thank your mentors, bosses, colleagues and anyone who contributes to your success. Be specific. But most of all, be redundant. If there's one thing to be obnoxious about, it's showing honest, sincere appreciation.

This resource is available as a free download at www.nathanmagnuson.com/resources.

BONUS #2

Decision-Making Hacks for Young Professionals

What is your comfort level in making big decisions? More importantly, what is the quality of your decisions? Do you get the outcome you want?

If you're a young professional, this really matters! Clinical psychologist Meg Jay notes in her book *The Defining Decade* that eighty percent of life's most defining moments happen before age 35.[38] Young professionals make some of the biggest decisions of their lives, many for the first time, while they're still decision-making novices!

That's why I developed an additional resource *Decision-Making Hacks for Young Professionals*, to help you move forward despite uncertainty. If you want to make quality decisions with confidence and efficiency, this resource is for you.

This resource is available as a free download at www.nathanmagnuson.com/resources.

BONUS #3

5 Ways to Win the Hearts of Your Young Professionals (For Leaders)

How will you attract, engage, develop and retain your young professionals?

Research produced by Bersin and Gallup show that despite organizations collectively investing over $700 million toward employee engagement initiatives each year[39], 55% of young professionals remain unengaged at work[40] – and many of them are looking to pursue outside opportunities.

Young professionals make up the largest segment of the workforce, which means the costs for low engagement and high turnover are astronomical. The battle to win the hearts of your young professionals, then, is a battle for your organization's health, financial success and long-term survival.

Fortunately, it's possible to win the hearts of your young professionals. I share the critical strategies in my white paper *5 Ways to Win the Hearts of Your Young Professionals.*

This white paper is available as a free download at www.nathanmagnuson.com/resources.

Also by Nathan Magnuson – Ignite Your Leadership Expertise

How would you like to be the next leadership expert? Even more, how would you like others to value and seek your input? It's well within you reach, *even if you're a new, young or relatively inexperienced leader*.

Drawing on over a decade of leadership and consulting experiences, Nathan Magnuson shares how to identify the leadership expertise you already possess, how to proactively and strategically develop it for deeper impact and how to confidently share it with others in a way that keeps them coming back for more.

The world is crying out for positive leadership examples to follow. Will you accept the challenge?

Order *Ignite Your Leadership Expertise* on Amazon.com or at *www.nathanmagnuson.com/ignite-your-leadership-expertise.*

Acknowledgements

Like most projects worth doing, this one required a team effort. I'd like to thank the following individuals for all their help and support.

Dan Miller, Mark Miller, Eric Evans, John G. Miller, Christopher Tuff, Daniel Jacobs, Janet Kamerman, Bob Thomas, Bob Tiede, Dave Kingsley, Jeff Myers and Doris Gomez – Your endorsements were incredible and really touched me! I'm humbled and grateful. Thank you.

Cassy Van Dyke, Chris Hendrix, Garland Vance, Kevin Sikes and Brian Lee – Thank you for your peer review feedback on my early drafts. Your feedback helped make this book much better!

Corrie Magnuson and Nichole Vaux - Thank you for your very helpful design input.

William Parker – Thank you for taking these words and turning them into a sharp looking book.

Nick Lee – Thank you for doing an incredible job with the book cover. You're a true artist!

Becky Robinson and the team at Weaving Influence – Thank you for all your help with the marketing plan. I'm so glad we finally got to work together!

Courtney Southerby and Abigail Linhardt – Thank you each for your careful copy-editing and proofreading. (I resisted the urge to put a typo in that sentence! ☺)

Launch Team – Thank you to everyone who participated on my launch team and helped share this book's message. You've helped make a difference for the folks who read this book.

Notes

Chapter 1

1. Stephen R. Covey, *The 7 Habits of Highly Effective People* (Mango, 2017). For more about Stephen R. Covey, visit: https://www.nathanmagnuson.com/leadership-profile-stephen-covey.
2. John Maxwell, *The 15 Invaluable Laws of Growth* (Center Street, 2014).
3. Zig Ziglar, *Developing the Qualities of Success* (Made for Success, Inc, 2008). For more about Zig Ziglar, visit: https://www.nathanmagnuson.com/leadership-profile-zig-ziglar.

Chapter 2

4. Joel Stein, *Time*, "Millennials: The Me Me Me Generation." (May 20, 2013). http://time.com/247/millennials-the-me-me-me-generation/.
5. Paul Angone, "3 Ways to Cure Obsessive Comparison Disorder," *All Groan Up*, accessed April 15, 2019, http://allgroanup.com/featured/obsessive-comparison-disorder/.
6. Nathan Magnuson, *LinkedIn Pulse*, "3 Lessons on Success from Jim Carrey," March 7, 2019. https://www.linkedin.com/pulse/3-lessons-success-from-jim-carrey-nathan-magnuson/.
7. Patrick Lencioni, *The Ideal Team Player* (Jossey-Bass, 2016).
8. Zig Ziglar, *Developing the Qualities of Success* (Made for Success, Inc, 2008). For more about Zig Ziglar, visit: https://www.nathanmagnuson.com/leadership-profile-zig-ziglar.

Chapter 3

9. Jim Carrey, Maharishi University of Management class of 2014 commencement address, accessed October 23, 2019. (accessed October 23, 2019). https://www.youtube.com/watch?v=V80-gPkpH6M.
10. Tom Rath, *StrengthsFinder 2.0* (Gallup Press, 2007).
11. The simplest way to complete the StrengthsFinder® assessment is to order the book *Strengths Based Leadership* by Tom Rath and Barry Conchie (Gallup Press, 2008) and utilize the code included in the back.

Chapter 4

12. LinkedIn (2016), *2016 Global Talent Trends*. LinkedIn. https://business.linkedin.com/talent-solutions/job-trends/2016-talent-trends-home/2016-global-talent-trends#.
13. Laura Vogel, Trulia, "The Place Generation" (June 18, 2018). https://www.trulia.com/blog/the-place-generation/.

Chapter 5

14. Ryan Jenkins, *The Millennial Manual* (Ryan Jenkins, 2017).
15. Kevin Carroll, *Rules of the Red Rubber Ball* (ESPN, 2005).
16. Jon Acuff, *Quitter* (Ramsey Press, 2015).

Chapter 6

17. Robert J. Thomas, *Crucibles of Leadership* (Harvard Business Review Press, 2008). For more on "crucibles," visit: https://www.nathanmagnuson.com/how-leaders-learn-to-lead/.
18. Nathan Magnuson, *NathanMagnuson.com*, "How

Leaders Learn to Lead" (June 5, 2017). https://www.nathanmagnuson.com/how-leaders-learn-to-lead/.

19. Nathan Magnuson, *NathanMagnuson.com*, "How to Get Great Feedback" (May 5, 2014). https://www.nathanmagnuson.com/how-to-get-great-feedback/.

Chapter 7

20. Mark Emmons, *Dynamic Signal*, "Key Statistics About Millennials in the Workplace," accessed August 3, 2019. https://dynamicsignal.com/2018/10/09/key-statistics-millennials-in-the-workplace/.
21. "How Millennials Want to Work and Live," *Gallup*, 2016. https://www.gallup.com/workplace/238073/millennials-work-live.aspx.
22. John Maxwell, *The 15 Invaluable Laws of Growth* (Center Street, 2014).

Chapter 8

23. Nathan Magnuson, *NathanMagnuson.com*, "The 5 SOF Truths of Leadership" (July 22, 2013). https://www.nathanmagnuson.com/the-5-sof-truths-of-leadership/.
24. Mike Krzyzewski, *Leading with the Heart*. Warner Business Books, March 1, 2001.
25. Cheryl Bachelder, *Dare to Serve* (Berrett-Koehler Publishers, 2018).
26. Nathan Magnuson, *NathanMagnuson.com*, "Coach K: Mike Krzyzewski on Teamwork" (February 2, 2015). https://www.nathanmagnuson.com/coach-k-mike-krzyzewski-on-teamwork/.

Chapter 9

27. Nathan Magnuson, *Ignite Your Leadership Expertise* (Nathan Magnuson, 2018).
28. Ibid.

Chapter 10

29. Max De Pree, *Leadership is an Art* (Currency, 2004).
30. My book *Ignite Your Leadership Expertise* contains an entire chapter contrasting great and poor questions and sharing how to improve one's ability to ask high quality questions.
31. Shana Lebowitz, *Business Insider*, "The CEO of Popeyes says one of her biggest professional successes 'would not exist' if she hadn't been fired earlier in her career." (December 11, 2016). https://www.businessinsider.com/cheryl-bachelder-ceo-popeyes-2016-12.
32. Jonathan Maze, *Nation's Restaurant News*, "Cheryl Bachelder to Step Down at Popeye's." (March 2, 2017). https://www.nrn.com/people/cheryl-bachelder-step-down-popeyes.
33. "State of the American Workplace," *Gallup*, 2017. https://www.gallup.com/workplace/238085/state-american-workplace-report-2017.aspx.
34. Nathan Magnuson, *Ignite Your Leadership Expertise* (Nathan Magnuson, 2018).
35. Robert J. Thomas, *Crucibles of Leadership* (Harvard Business Review Press, 2008). For more on "crucibles," visit: https://www.nathanmagnuson.com/how-leaders-learn-to-lead/.

Bonus Content

36. Nathan Magnuson, *NathanMagnuson.com*, "Leadership Profile: Jack Welch," (October 7, 2013). https://www.nathanmagnuson.com/leadership-profile-jack-welch/.
37. Nathan Magnuson, *NathanMagnuson.com*, "More Smiles, More Dollars," (June 4, 2018). https://www.nathanmagnuson.com/more-smiles-more-dollars/.
38. Meg Jay, *The Defining Decade* (Twelve, 2012).
39. "Employee Engagement: Market Review, Buyer's Guide and Provider Profiles," Bersin, 2012. http://www.bersin.com/engagement-market-review.
40. "How Millennials Want to Work and Live," *Gallup*, 2016. https://www.gallup.com/workplace/238073/millennials-work-live.aspx.

About Nathan

Nathan Magnuson is a leadership and young professional expert and serves as a consultant, coach and speaker for corporate audiences. He's worked in a staff or consulting role with many Fortune 500 companies and large public service organizations, including Accenture, MASCO, FBI and Defense Intelligence Agency, among others. Nathan is also a military veteran, having served with the Army Special Operations in Operation Iraqi Freedom.

In addition to corporate work, Nathan is also an active author, having written the books *Stand Out!* and *Ignite Your Leadership Expertise*. Nathan's articles and resources are posted on his website NathanMagnuson.com and in various leadership publications.

You can follow Nathan on Facebook, Twitter, LinkedIn or on his website. To inquire about speaking, consulting or coaching for young professional initiatives, contact nathan@nathanmagnuson.com.

www.facebook.com/NathanMagnusonLeadership

www.twitter.com/nathanmagnuson

www.linkedin.com/in/nathanmagnuson

Recommended Reading

Leadership

- *Ignite Your Leadership Expertise* by Nathan Magnuson
- *How to Win Friends and Influence People* by Dale Carnegie
- *The 7 Habits of Highly Effective People* by Stephen R. Covey
- *Dare to Serve* by Cheryl Bachelder
- *Switch* by Chip Heath & Dan Heath
- *Good to Great* by Jim Collins
- *The Secret* by Ken Blanchard & Mark Miller
- *Extreme Ownership* by Jocko Willink & Leif Babin
- *The 21 Irrefutable Laws of Leadership* by John Maxwell
- *Start with Why* by Simon Sinek
- *Leading with the Heart* by Mike Krzyzewski & Donald Phillips
- *Leadership and Self-Deception* by The Arbinger Institute
- *Creativity, Inc.* by Ed Catmull
- *Great Leaders Grow* by Ken Blanchard & Mark Miller
- *The Five Dysfunctions of a Team* by Patrick Lencioni
- *Crucial Conversations* by Kerry Patterson, Joseph Grenny, Ron McMillan & Al Switzler
- *The 15 Invaluable Laws of Growth* by John Maxwell

Career

- *48 Days to the Work You Love* by Dan Miller
- *No More Dreaded Mondays* by Dan Miller
- *What Color is Your Parachute?* by Richard Bolles
- *Quitter* by Jon Acuff

Life

- *Rules of the Red Rubber Ball* by Kevin Carroll
- *Let Your Life Speak* by Parker Palmer
- *QBQ! The Question Behind the Question* by John G. Miller
- *Decisive* by Chip Heath & Dan Heath
- *How to Stop Worrying and Start Living* by Dale Carnegie
- *Rejection Proof* by Jia Jiang
- *Start* by Jon Acuff

Made in the USA
Middletown, DE
15 November 2020

24070079R10076